BLINDSIDED

ALSO BY JIM COLE

Lives of Grizzlies: Alaska
Lives of Grizzlies: Montana and Wyoming

BLINDSIDED

Surviving a Grizzly Attack and
Still Loving the Great Bear

Jim Cole
with Tim Vandehey

ST. MARTIN'S PRESS ≋ NEW YORK

www.stmartins.com

Book design by Phil Mazzone

Library of Congress Cataloging-in-Publication Data

Cole, Jim.
    Blindsided : surviving a grizzly attack and still loving the great bear / Jim Cole with Tim Vandehey—1st ed.
          p. cm.
   ISBN 978-0-312-60109-6
   1. Grizzly bear—Yellowstone National Park.   2. Bear attacks—Yellowstone National Park.   3. Grizzly bear—Behavior.   4. Cole, Jim—Health.   I. Vandehey, Tim.   II. Title.
   QL737.C27C629 2010
   599.784092—dc22
   [B]

                          2009045704

First Edition: June 2010

10   9   8   7   6   5   4   3   2   1

Dedicated to Ron and Richard

My life is a tribute to my father,
Robert Charles Cole, aka Bobby Cohen.

CONTENTS

ACKNOWLEDGMENTS

Heartfelt appreciation goes out to: Lisa Sharkey for being such a great advocate and friend—thanks for believing in me from the very beginning; my literary agent, Sharlene Martin, for her tenacious attitude and creative guidance; Andrea Beaumont for her insight and unwavering support from early on; my wonderful editor, Daniela Rapp, for her perceptive wisdom and vision in crafting this book; my friend Tim Vandehey for all the patience, creativity, hard work, baseball talk, and good old common sense.

ACKNOWLEDGMENTS

My undying gratitude goes out to Dr. Hinckley, Dr. Durborow, Dr. Krell, Dr. Whatmore, Nancy Brown, nurses "Tall Paul," Robyn, Deb, Ryan, Glenn, Rocky, and any other EIRMC folks whose names escaped me in the fog. Special thanks to Richard the security guard who gave us some needed peace of mind. Words can't express how much I owe you all for giving me back my sight and my life.

I wouldn't be writing this book without the incredible gifts from my father, my mother, my sister Tootsie, John and Judy Taylor, Judy Geiger, Molly Kiser, Elle Berman, Bill Edelman, Merle Watson, my dog Merle, and of course Richard and Ron, the greatest friends ever. I love you all.

BLINDSIDED

INTRODUCTION

It's the last wild country, the grizzly calls home
Following his nose through the kingdom he roams
Resourceful and wary, as smart as you get
Bears learn quickly and never forget

—"Wonderful World," music and lyrics by James R. Cole

IT WAS THE SUMMER of 1960. I was a ten-year-old sports fanatic from Chicago, passing my first summer, as so many other young boys have done, at Camp Menominee in the lake-dense woods of northern Wisconsin. But I wasn't like a lot of other boys my age, who tend to be all scabs and skinned knees. I was a good athlete, and I was excited about a summer playing sports. I thought the highlight of the summer would be winning a tennis tournament. Boy, was I wrong.

I don't remember the date, but I will never forget when the startled young black bear bolted out from the dense forest into the camp's tennis complex. From the bruin's confused perspective, the scene couldn't have made much sense: clean-cut ten-year-old boys in tennis shorts with matching T-shirts were running in every direction hitting fuzzy round objects toward each other with strange sticks. For my part, I froze and stared, unsure if this was really happening. I was a suburban kid; wildlife for me consisted of the scavenging raccoons my dad would chase away from our back porch, swinging a broomstick while trying to look like Steve McQueen but ending up looking more like Groucho Marx. I could barely believe what I was seeing. A bear. Up close. Out of the woods, just like that.

Back then I didn't know much about bears, but one thing was obvious: this big animal was familiar with the concept of the shortest distance between two points being a straight line. Clearly eager to get out of the company of humans as quickly as possible, it abruptly made a beeline straight across the tennis courts without a moment's hesitation, directly toward the timber that lined the far edge of the courts. Frightened, excited, and confused boys scattered everywhere, giving this fish-out-of-water black bear a wide berth. In what must have been just a few seconds, the ghostly bruin disappeared just as quickly as he had emerged. As far as anyone knew, he was never seen again at camp that summer.

I recall that I was unreasonably frightened of the bear, although I had no idea why. When he bolted for the woods (headed "right for me," as my panicked brain was insisting) my first instinct was to take the fastest route out of harm's way—in this case, the high fence that divided the tennis courts. Unfortunately, I was an inept climber. I lurched and bumbled my way toward the top of the fence, eight or maybe ten feet from the ground, then risked a glance over my shoulder, half certain the bruin would be following me up the fence (which he easily could have done; they are adept climbers) with red eyes and slavering jaws. To my relief (and some embarrassment), the bear had raced by me without so much as a glance. Hindsight and experience tell me now that the bear simply wanted to remove himself from this surprising, unfamiliar, and potentially dangerous environment as quickly as possible. He had stumbled across this scene by chance and hadn't intended to create mayhem.

I don't know why I was so afraid of bears. In my mind, I think they tripped a purely instinctive panic response, accompanied by deep-seated mental images of bears as vicious and dangerous, with the very real potential to attack humans at any time. But in reality, I did not know anything about bears other than my stuffed bear, Joe, whose torn-up body resides in a pillowcase in my bedroom closet to this day. In the end, the visitor was the talk of the mess hall that night, but for most of the kids the event was just another cool camp memory to be carried forward through the years.

For me, it was a seed.

At that time in my young life, I wouldn't have known the difference between a black bear and a wolverine. My sister was the animal nut. I, on the other hand, was afraid of the beagle puppy, Mike, that my parents brought home. For some reason, the word "beagle" sounded intimidating to me and I hid upstairs in my room as my parents and sister gathered around him in our front yard. My wildlife viewing in my early years was limited to deer, tree squirrels gathering nuts in our suburban backyard, a potpourri of birds, and raccoons raiding the backyard trash even after my father installed sunken garbage cans to discourage them. One time, a raccoon pup fell into one of the sunken garbage pails and cried out from its underground trap while the helpless mom and two siblings stood close by. With a broom in his left hand, wearing pajama shorts, a T-shirt, and slippers, my dad faced off with the snarling mother, holding her at bay with the broom until he was finally able to lift the can to free the frightened ringtail.

I was the pig-headed, stubborn, adventurous son of two great parents who gave me virtually unlimited freedom to cruise our Chicagoland neighborhood on my black one-speed Schwinn bicycle. I wasn't a budding naturalist; I was a sports nut. My world revolved around the Chicago pro sports teams, particularly the White Sox in baseball, the Bears in football, and the Blackhawks in hockey. I seem to remember sitting in class in 1959 when the Sox played the Los Angeles Dodgers in their first World Series in four decades, listening to the game with a radio earphone cord secretly running up my shirt sleeve, hearing Bob Shaw pitch a 1–0 shutout in Game Five to beat a little-known pitcher by the name of Sandy Koufax. Sports was life for me; wildlife, not so much.

When I was a child, my family took many excursions to

the Lincoln Park Zoo. I recall gripping my great grandfather's huge hand as I entered the antiquated, smelly lion house for the first time. Loud roars echoed off the walls and were deafening at times. If ever I saw grizzly or black bears at this zoo, I do not remember them. My other exposure to wildlife was the weekly television show *Wild Kingdom,* which I watched religiously. As I did, secret dreams filtered through my mind and my heart yearned to be in the wild, sharing adventures with Marlin Perkins and Jim Fowler. During the commercials I'd be smiling, shaking my head, and thinking to myself, "What incredibly exciting lives they must lead." At the time, I think I was more comfortable seeing animals on television or in zoos than I was being around them in real life. Clearly that would change.

Despite my typical city boy upbringing, by age twelve it became apparent to me that I wasn't comfortable with my surroundings. I was restless, but for what I didn't know. In hindsight, my Wisconsin wilderness experience gave me far more than the honor of being heralded as a softball or tennis star. It opened my eyes to a new and wild world. I was realizing that the boreal forest of the Upper Midwest was a wildlife mecca. The abundant wildlife of the area, which was largely ignored by most campers and counselors, entranced me. I was constantly trying to finagle more wildlife observation opportunities.

My early naked-eye observations of Sand Lake, near the camp, quickly taught me the difference between raptor fishing styles. Bald eagles sank only their talons and yellow legs into the water to grab fish near the surface, while ospreys plunged their entire wings and bodies into the lake, then slowly regained altitude as water scattered off their drenched feathers. Deer were common as well as frogs and snakes. The dense timber was alive with creatures lurking in the shadows. At night, unidentified animal sounds echoed through the darkened woods that surrounded camp. In the summers after my bear encounter, my dad and I often took slow nighttime drives along the roads from northern Wisconsin through Michigan's Upper Peninsula looking for "wildlife eyes" along the road. We saw mostly deer with an occasional porcupine, opossum, or skunk.

Back in those days, many people hated and feared the food chain-topping predators of the North American wilderness: the bear, mountain lion, and wolf. These city folk had no idea of the predator's critical role in a well-balanced, healthy ecosystem. Neither did the government. Most folks only knew what they saw or read in the news, which, to my growing outrage, only focused on the rare human attack or nuisance extermination of wolves or coyotes. But while most people I knew regarded the wild lands with fear and misunderstanding, I was fascinated. There was also some fear, but fascination quickly took over and crowded out the fear. Then my life moved on to college, career, and financial pursuits, and that seed lay dormant for years. But it was just biding its time.

The mother grizzly stood on her hind legs and looked directly toward us with her intense brown eyes. My sister, Tootsie, and

I sat silently in my one-ton orange 1963 Chevy panel truck as two furry blond yearling cubs followed their mom's lead, warily glaring in our direction. After that one thoughtful look, this magnificent bear family, bearing their lush winter coats, bolted uphill and quickly vanished, swallowed up by the dense timber. It was a brief moment, but it changed everything for me.

This single sighting in November 1975 in Glacier National Park sent my mind into a whirlwind of thoughts and questions about the animal that I was already most fascinated with, the grizzly bear. I had seen a multitude of television shows about the grizzly, but what was true? Were they really bloodthirsty man-killers? I was well aware of the fact that grizzlies rarely attacked humans but with all the informal research I had previously done, it was obvious that relatively little was known about these wary and secretive creatures.

After that, the seed that had been planted by my fence-climbing bear encounter so long ago began to sprout in a big way. I began to frequent Glacier and Yellowstone Parks but rarely saw grizzlies. When I did, it was usually from great distances or just their retreating hindquarters. Then I spoke to a naturalist in Jasper National Park in Canada who recognized that I had a keen interest in wildlife. He confided to me that the only real way to learn about an animal's life was to safely follow it to get a firsthand look at "what it eats, where it travels, and how it interacts with other animals." I never forgot that advice.

Gradually, even as I began what would become a lucrative

career in real estate, my life reached the point where I was voracious about learning everything that I could about the lives of grizzly bears. These animals are at the top of the food chain and their very existence in the contiguous United States is in peril due to development, habitat loss, and the increasing encroachment of human activities. The more I studied the great bear, the more apparent it became how untrue the myths and perceptions were.

I am a passionate person to begin with, and as the years went by, my passion to uncover the true nature of the grizzly only grew. I wanted to document natural grizzly behavior and interactions with humans in as many different ecosystems as I could. Although roadside viewing is valuable and informative, it seemed very limiting and I knew that I had to walk the land with the great bear. As a boy, I often dreamed of hitting the winning home run in the seventh game of the World Series, but this was different. This was realistic. To make it happen, I have hiked over 27,000 miles in grizzly country from Wyoming to Alaska. I wanted to get inside of the bear's head as much as is humanly possible.

My travels have taken me to eleven different grizzly bear ecosystems and I have documented many of my observations, experiences, and photographs in two other published books. I have lived out my dream of observing grizzly bears in the wild in some of the most beautiful places in the world. In my travels, I have observed grizzlies in ten different months and have seen fresh grizzly tracks every month of the year.

In the winter of 2008, I had the rare opportunity to see a

grizzly consuming a wolf-killed elk in Yellowstone on December 23 and 24; this was by far my greatest holiday gift ever. The big grizzly guarded and fed on the cow elk carcass on December 23rd. Light snow fell all day as the temperature never rose above six degrees Fahrenheit in northern Yellowstone country. Wolves had killed this elk a couple of days earlier in an open meadow about 125 yards north of the park road, but they were nowhere to be seen that day. In typical grizzly fashion, the bear buried the carcass with grasses after each meal to disguise the smell from potential competition, although I doubt that there was any animal around who could have seriously challenged him. Three different coyotes pilfered small morsels but the bruin never ventured more than a few feet from his prize, even taking naps right on top of this mound of meat. When grizzlies are active this late in the year, it's usually the big males and this guy likely tipped the scale at over 400 pounds.

The following day, Christmas Eve, the snow continued and the bear still controlled the scene, flanked only by opportunistic ravens and magpies. No sign of coyotes. Very little meat remained as he turned the bones over and over, consuming every last morsel of flesh between naps. Late in the afternoon, snow flew up with every step as he made his exit through the deep white powder. This was the latest in the year that I have ever seen a grizzly and it was a truly special sight to behold.

I am one of the luckiest men on earth. To my knowledge, nobody else has experienced grizzlies in the ways that I have, from such a unique and broad perspective. I did not limit myself to any one single geographic region as this animal survives in many different areas in many different ways, depending on climate, the variety of natural foods available, and the degree of tolerance and understanding, or lack thereof, from humans.

In 1990, I walked away from a lucrative business career, fortunate enough to have a moderate nest egg, and relocated to West Glacier, Montana, near Glacier National Park. Since then, I have financed my own studies using my writing, teaching, and my skills as a songwriter and musician (not to mention sleeping many nights in my vehicle to conserve money) so as not to be directed by or beholden to anyone. I've never been one to follow along with the crowd. On the other hand, I don't do things just to be different. This wasn't just about becoming a temporary mountain man. What I do is something that rises from the deepest part of who and what I am. It *is* who and what I am.

I have lost too many family members and friends at young ages, and this realization motivated me to live out my dreams while I still had my health and my drive. After I saw those first grizzlies in 1975, my life's path gradually became clear. I didn't want to pursue a profession only to make money, then grow old reflecting on what might have been. I wanted to make a significant contribution to other people's lives. One of my great idols was Jackie Robinson, who once said: "A life is not important except in the impact it has on other lives." It's on his gravestone in Brooklyn. I live by that maxim, and I want to do everything I can to protect the grizzlies and the remaining wilderness where they live.

Part of my mission is also a desire to share what I know with others by incorporating my deep passion for teaching into my work. I have come to learn that the sensational myths about these animals are grossly untrue and it has become my mission to reveal this to the public through my books, public education programs, music, and photographic documentation. I want to turn everything I have seen and done into educational material, get the opportunity to go into the public schools and other venues, appear in the media, and educate people. I want them to understand how little habitat there is left. I don't think many people east of the Mississippi really get it. The power we have to create or destroy is epic. I will stay out in the field as long as my health lets me, but the great thing is even after my knees or my back or my eyesight tell me that twenty-five mile day hikes are no longer in the cards, I should have decades left to teach.

That's not to say my decision to drop out of the rat race and dedicate my life to studying the great bear hasn't been without cost and sacrifice. Even setting aside the fact that I've been mauled twice, I have paid a price for following my passion. I've never had children, and I think I would have made a great father. I thrive on personal relationships, but my social interaction has been constricted by the contrast between my life among humans and my life among bears. I sometimes feel lonely and isolated on extended backcountry field trips, especially when the weather is harsh. These experiences are often humbling and help to ground me with a stronger appreciation for the basic amenities that most of us take for granted in everyday life. But I don't have any regrets. I've always felt that the most important things in life are family, friends, and having or creating the time to do things that are most important to you. I have never been a materialistic person. I don't have much of tangible value other than my camera equipment and musical instruments. My wealth is that I am fortunate enough to spend some of my time with my family and friends and the rest doing what I love.

When I walk the earth with the great bear, I come alive. I'm a physical, athletic guy and I love hiking in the clear air, knowing that I'm doing something great for my body and taking in some of the most gorgeous country on earth. On my own in the wild, I just breathe in the subtleties of nature. In the winter of 2008, I was cross-country skiing in the early morning light with two inches of fresh snow on the ground, and I knew that tracking would be ideal. About four miles into the backcountry, I came across the fresh tracks of a pair of coyotes traveling ahead of me in the same direction. They followed the trail for about a half-mile before heading down a steep slope and into the timber. They may have heard me coming. Reading animal sign is fascinating as stories are written in the whiteness of winter. Even when you don't see the animals, it's fun to know that they're around and to figure out what they're doing.

I relish everything about what I do: learning, educating,

hiking, observing, and photographing. After almost losing my life in 2007, it was important to get back to what I do and I feel very fortunate that I've been able to accomplish that. I was not about to give in to my injuries if I had the strength within me.

That brings me to the subjects of fear and craziness. When people find out what I do and what I've experienced, many of them ask me if I'm afraid of the grizzly bear now, or if I'm nuts to still be out there in bear country. Because of public and media interest in my maulings, these incidents (particularly the most recent one) perpetuate fear in the minds of the uneducated. No doubt they've heard of Timothy Treadwell, the "Grizzly Man" of the movie of the same name, and think I'm headed for his kind of sad and gruesome death.

To these kinds of questions, I can only say that when I do something important, I dive in headfirst. Nothing halfway. When I was playing high school tennis, I outworked everybody. I wasn't the best player, but I became number one because of my work ethic. When I walked onto my college tennis team, nobody gave me a shot, but I never lost a tennis match because the other person was in better shape or because I wore out. When I do my marathon backcountry hikes, it's difficult but I may push myself to do thirty miles instead of twenty-five. Is it worth it? You're damned right it is. When it comes to the things I care about, I'm compulsive and driven.

My life with grizzlies is the same way, although in the

beginning I really had no idea what I was getting myself into. Now that I do, I wouldn't change a thing. I have realized that the more I learn about these incredible animals, the more I realize how much I don't know. It's humbling; my learning curve continues to rise even after all these many years of first-hand wilderness experience. So I can honestly say that even after being mauled once in 1993 and much more seriously in 2007, I really don't consider what I do to be unusually dangerous. My maulings were surprise encounters where, in each case, the bear saw me before I saw it. Also, with the extraordinary time I spend out in grizzly country, the odds of me having a mishap are far greater than the average person's. Anybody can be in the wrong place at the wrong time. But I have a great understanding of bear behavior and feel very comfortable walking on their turf. Even after all that has happened, I feel at home as much as ever in grizzly country.

You take a greater risk driving to work every day than I do observing a 300-pound mother grizzly and her cubs alone in the wilderness. What happened to me was like being struck by lightning twice; you can't spend the rest of your life hiding in the house when it rains. Rather than fear, I feel a sense of honor and duty to continue doing what I do. My work has always felt like an important and worthy endeavor but now more than ever. In light of the 2007 attack, it's even more important now that I speak out and continue speaking out, letting people know the true, complex, subtle, intelligent, and majestic nature of these animals.

On one afternoon in Glacier Park several years ago, I was

sitting in my van watching a black bear running at full speed to the east to get away from a grizzly that was casually foraging in a thicket of serviceberries. The frightened black bear ran directly across the Apikuni Trail close behind two oblivious hikers who were deep in conversation as they neared the trailhead. The bear continued its sprint and disappeared into thick cover. I never did see the grizzly come out of the dense serviceberry patch. The young couple never saw either bear.

When they reached the trailhead, I told them what had just happened and they were shocked. But we shared a good laugh about it as well. The bears that were in the area had not been the bloodthirsty killing machines that so many people see lurking behind every tree in the Mountain West. They had been completely unconcerned about the nearby humans and were just going about their own business. So to my mind, it's not the grizzly that needs to change its attitude toward us. It's the other way around.

As the subtitle of this book suggests, I still love the great bear—perhaps more now than ever. The 1993 attack didn't change my feelings about them. I wanted to get back on the horse. By the time the field season started the next spring, I was ready to go. The only change was that I carried two cans of bear spray instead of one. The 2007 attack was different, if only because I was older and at first there was some question of my surviving. The attack was also a little harder on my psyche; my first night awake after three days in a sedated coma, I had vivid nightmares and dreamed the bear was in the hospital room. But that was all.

If anything, being attacked and surviving has made my feelings and resolve stronger. I know that sounds crazy to someone who doesn't have that kind of passion, but it's true. My affection for the bears was so strong to begin with that nothing could have diminished it. Getting back out into the field after the second attack wasn't a question of fear or desire, but of capability.

But once I was back in Glacier and Yellowstone for my first fieldwork since the attack, I knew everything would be fine. Later in Alaska, there were bears all around me, and because I now have a blind spot on one side, you would think I would be especially vulnerable, but at no time did I feel that way. It struck me that the level of my skills and knowledge of bear country substituted for my lost vision. Because I knew many of the individual bears over multiple generations and had so much experience with them, my mind could usually predict their behavior patterns as accurately as if I had the use of both eyes. I found myself as comfortable as ever. It was like riding a bicycle.

So in the wake of being mauled, blinded, and left for dead, my appreciation for everything has actually been enhanced. Because now I am not 100 percent, I have begun to appreciate my awareness and understanding of the bear and its habitat more than ever before. I had one of my best field seasons in 2008, especially given my age and limitations. I did everything that year that I would normally do, including hiking over 2,300 backcountry miles. Of course, one of the reasons I pushed myself was to prove that I could still do it. It was unbelievably gratifying to find that I still could, and to realize that I was back out in grizzly country as fearless and enthusiastic as before, still cherishing every moment in the beautiful country with the great bears.

This feeling is not just about the bear—it's also about what the bear represents. The bear represents true wilderness, what used to be—wild lands, the wild part of us and our connection with nature. If grizzlies live in an ecosystem, you're going to have a healthier wilderness, and the other rare animals in the system, such as lynx and wolverine, can thrive. Grizzly bears are a barometer; healthy populations usually mean healthy country.

And it's all in danger of being lost. People tell me all the time that I'm fighting a losing battle—that in the end the sprawl of development and progress will win. That drives me past fear and pain and isolation more powerfully than anything else. The grizzly is an incredibly intelligent, interesting creature with endless facets—an animal that, unless you know that individual bear, is capable of humbling you and doing things you don't expect. Any grizzly you don't know is as surprising and individual as any human being you don't know. To think that through our own shortsightedness and ignorance we could wipe such a creature off the earth . . . to me, as much as I treasure these animals, that would be an unimaginable catastrophe.

I think the grizzly's existence is a testimonial to our own existence. If we can't preserve and protect the animal and the wilderness, how are we going to preserve and protect ourselves? What drives me to go back into the wild to track the great bear after nearly losing my life to it twice? It's the hope that enhanced awareness will bring a new era of hope for greater conservation. I always want to be hopeful. When I have voted in the past, the environment was one of my major issues. In the last two presidential elections, it was rarely mentioned. But if we see the environment as a luxury, we're done for. The situation is precarious. You can fight for years to preserve a wilderness, but all it takes is one loss and it's gone forever.

I feel indebted to the grizzly bear and the American wilderness for what they have done for my life. Dedicating my life to learning about them and sharing that knowledge is repayment of that debt. My eyesight? I suppose that's the interest I had to pay. But it will be ultimately worth it if I can continue to help other people and their children to see what I've seen—grizzly bears in the wilderness of Glacier, Alaska, and Yellowstone. An informed public will create more support for grizzly habitat, and will help create an enlightened image of the bear that's based on knowledge, love, and respect, not fear. If people can hear the perspective of someone who's been out there and experienced things—even dangerous things—I believe it can change their perspectives. I hope I can inspire them to take a few steps on the path toward loving and venerating this great animal . . . as I continue to do.

1

My First Attack

With fear as the fabric woven in mystery
Generations pass down sensational folklore
Now hikers are yelling with cow bells and air horns
And leaving their common sense parked at the door.

—"Bearanoia," music and lyrics by James R. Cole

I NEVER SAW THE young grizzly that tore a hole in my head until he was a few feet from attacking me. All I knew was that I faced a ten-and-a-half-mile hike to save my own life. It was good training for what was to happen in 2007.

September 29, 1993, was a gorgeous Indian summer day in Glacier National Park, my favorite place in the world. I had been living in the area since 1991 after turning my back on my real estate career. The change had given me everything I had hoped it would: the complete freedom to study animals in their natural habitats, a release from what had become a high-stress lifestyle, and most important, the opportunity to experience grizzly bears in one of the most stunningly beautiful places on earth. I was like a kid in a candy store.

Just a few years earlier, when real estate had been my bread and butter, I was always tethered to business. Even when taking vacation time to hike the backcountry, I would regularly check in with my office out of that ridiculous idea people have that if they're not handling every tiny detail the world will stop turning. Now Glacier was my home, and I had no obligations other than to pursue my passion, the business of the grizzly bear. I could take backpacking and hiking trips whenever I wanted. After spending the summer in Alaska, I couldn't wait to get back to the park and keep my finger on the pulse of this ecosystem. To do that, I had to pound out the backcountry miles; Glacier makes you work for your bear sightings.

The season was winding down as the early winter that descends on the Big Sky backcountry was nearly upon us, but that day was stunning: flawless blue sky, the last of the fall color rustling in the trees, and temperatures in the seventies. My buddy Tim Rubbert and I wore shorts and T-shirts during the entire hike, normally unthinkable this late in the season. My sister and brother-in-law, along with our friend Molly, were arriving the next day, so I was looking forward to making one last major trek into grizzly country before the snow started to fly. I knew this was the day to get in a monster hike, the kind we both liked to do to test our fitness and also to see country that would become inaccessible to us when the winter descended. This was also an important time for the grizzly bears, because once snow begins to pile up on frozen ground, digging is not as easy. We expected at the very least to see signs of energetic foraging as the bruins tried to pack on weight for the cold, dark months ahead.

We had planned a twenty-five-mile round-trip hike to Fifty Mountain, the kind of grueling trip that most hikers would only tackle in multiple days. But years of carrying heavy gear deep into the wilderness to observe and photograph the majestic and awesome grizzly bear had gotten me in great shape; humping a forty-pound backpack and camera up and down relentless switchbacks for hours was a good workout but not a big deal. Fortuitously, I was wearing a shirt that said "Camp Menominee," the name of the camp where I had my first bear encounter. I'd stayed in touch with the camp over the years and they had sent me an updated version of what I wore when I was a camper there.

Tim and I were headed for the heart of one of the most majestic locations on the planet. Glacier National Park became a national park in 1910 after president William Howard Taft signed it into existence. It covers more than one million acres of pristine ecosystem and is home to two mountain ranges (the Lewis and the Livingston), a shrinking collection of glaciers, the famed Going-to-the-Sun Road, which crosses the Continental Divide at Logan Pass, and a dazzling array of wildlife including bighorn sheep, mountain goats, elk, moose, mountain lion, bald and golden eagles, black bear, wolf, the rare lynx and wolverine . . . and of course, the grizzly bear. The park is also simply one of the most breathtaking examples of what the natural world can look like when humans resist their call to "progress" and live lightly and respectfully on the land. Just being there is always a shot of adrenaline for me.

Aside from my joy at being back in the park, I was delighted at the prospect of spending the day with Tim, the closest thing I have to a kindred bear spirit. Tim is slim and fit, about six feet tall and bearded. His path was similar to mine: he left the insurance business to come up to northwestern Montana, live in grizzly country, and enjoy the freedom to hike, study, and explore. In the summer of 1991, my first summer of freedom, the annual Grizzly/Wolf Workshop was held along the north fork of the Flathead River near the northwest corner of Glacier National Park. People who were interested in the subject matter could come to this area, set up camp, and attend informal presentations by professional naturalists and biologists. Mike Fairchild, one of the wolf researchers I had lived with the previous winter, was leading a wolf field trip up near the Canadian border.

On the car ride to that trip, Mike was in the front seat and I was in the back, along with a character about my age. I noticed that not only did we have similar gear, he carried the identical camera holster, always keeping his camera in the ready position. We started to talk and discovered common interests, so we decided to get together and do some hiking. Things snowballed from there, and two years later we were ready to close out the 1993 Glacier season in fine style. Tim's a very animated, natural guy, and I've always found him to be funny by just being himself. He's blunt and direct; he doesn't put on airs or facades, and doesn't pull any punches. He lets you know what he thinks about things and where he stands. We understand each other well.

That morning, Tim and I set off before dawn so we could get on the trail at first light. Driving well into the interior of the park in the dark, we turned onto a dirt road to access the Packer's Roost trailhead. After a gear check, off we went. The trail up Flattop Mountain begins in the woods and switches back up the mountain through heavy underbrush. As you approach the summit, the trail rises beyond the timberline and into open country where a backpacker can see great distances. You can take out your binoculars and "glass" for miles, 360 degrees around. It is awesome.

The landscape opens up into a beautiful series of cascading meadows, surrounded by the great peaks and landmarks of the park: Heaven's Peak, Cathedral Peak, The Garden Wall, Iceberg Peak, Swiftcurrent Lookout, Longfellow Peak, and Vulture Peak. The view gives an incredible sense of the grandeur of the place. I remember that I felt lucky to be getting in one last challenging hike in such a gorgeous setting. I was planning to go hiking with my sister and family, but those hikes would be moderate. Few people had the stamina to keep up with me and Tim.

We were headed for Fifty Mountain campground, twelve miles in. The campground was closed for camping but the trail was open for day use, probably because the Park Service assumed that nobody in their right mind was going to try a twenty-five-mile round-trip day hike. As always, we had emergency gear and warm clothing in case we got stranded and were forced to spend the night, but the plan was to hike in, have lunch, and hike out.

Rangers had closed the campground because grizzlies had been frequenting the area and they didn't want people there overnight. Only after we climbed to a big open meadow about a half-mile above the campground and stopped for lunch did it become clear what the big omnivores had been up to. The meadows looked as though an army of oversized gophers from *Caddyshack* had gone ballistic on them. Grizzlies love a bright yellow native flower called the glacier lily, which blooms in the spring and which, by the way, is great in salads. In the fall, the bears are trying to pack on body weight for the winter hibernation period, and one of their favorite delicacies in this ecosystem is the energy-rich bulb, or corm, of the glacier lily. Grizzlies are incredible diggers, using their massive claws and that famous hump of muscle on their shoulders, and their prospecting for delicious corm was what made the landscape look like a fairway after an attack by a swarm of incompetent golfers. However, after thoroughly glassing in every direction for over a half hour, we didn't spot a single bruin.

Tim and I ate lunch in this rototilled meadow and remarked that not only had we not seen any bears on our hike in, we hadn't even seen any fresh bear sign—no scat, no tracks, no diggings, no urine trails. It was reasonable to assume that the unseasonably warm weather caused the bears to lay low during the heat of the day to conserve energy.

At any rate, the trail leading into this part of Glacier

National Park seemed to be bear-free, which may have made us a little complacent on our hike out. Never assume that if you see nothing on the hike in, you're not going to see something on the hike out.

When you're in bear country, it's advisable to make plenty of noise so the animals know you're coming. Bear attacks on humans are *extremely* rare, and most of them involve a hiker or camper catching a bear by surprise, often a mother with her cubs. That's why you'll see trekkers in bear territory wearing bells, carrying air horns, shaking a can full of rocks, yelling, or simply talking or singing loudly. Unless they are human-habituated or lured in by temptations like food left out at a campsite, bears will usually do anything to avoid confrontations with humans, so it's smart to give them as much advance warning as possible so they can give you a wide berth as you pass. Tim and I weren't doing enough of that, an error that would prove costly.

We finished our lunch and looked at the time: a little after 2 P.M. We knew if we wanted to reach the Packer's Roost trailhead before dark around 7 P.M., we needed to head out. So we shouldered our packs and headed back toward Flattop Mountain. We were walking on an open hillside dotted with subalpine fir trees, Tim continually scanning our surroundings with his binoculars all the way over to Highline Trail. I'm from Chicago and he's from Minneapolis, so we were riding each other about the White Sox, Twins, Bears, and Vikings, but as Tim hung back to get a better look at the prime grizzly habitat, I walked ten or fifteen yards ahead.

It was about 3:00 P.M. As I said, I never saw the bear in advance. I only heard a huffing, blowing sound (Tim said it was more like hissing) to my left, and saw the beautiful face of a sub-adult grizzly coming at me from only about ten feet away. The only logical scenario we could figure later was that after we had passed earlier that day, the bear had moved into the area and made itself a daybed in the small grove of trees beside the trail. If the bear had been up and about, we likely would have spotted it. Almost certainly, I had startled the bruin from its nap at close range and it instinctively attacked me in self-defense. It was a classic surprise encounter, not predation or an attempt to get our food.

I literally had no time to think about anything; all I did was instinctively react by dropping to the ground to protect my face and head. The attack was so quick that I didn't have time to even consider reaching for my bear spray. I certainly didn't have the time to feel fear.

That was small consolation as the 200-pound bear took a few clumsy roundhouse swings at me, missing as I fell to the ground and looking like, Tim said later, a drunken boxer. It did manage to tear open my scalp with its teeth, bite into my left wrist as I tried to shield my face, tear off the camera holster I keep at my left side, and then press me to the ground with its weight. I did the only thing I could do, which was to cover up as Tim came to my aid.

Looking back, I don't think the animal even realized there was another person on the trail, so intent was he on me. But as he had me pinned to the ground and I was trying not to move,

Tim took out his bear spray and fired a quick, loud burst that instantly got the grizzly's attention. I can't think of too many moments more worthy of the epithet, "Oh shit," than to see the great head of an angry grizzly bear suddenly swivel to find you standing thirty feet away with a can of bear spray in your hand. The bear bolted toward Tim, who unloaded virtually every bit of his spray directly into its face at close range. Finally, when the grizzly had closed to within about five feet of him, it caught the full force of the caustic spray and took a sharp detour down the slope, leaving us in shocked silence.

As I rose to my feet, I remember Tim asking me, "Jim, are you okay?" I don't recall any pain at that point; I was so charged with adrenaline that my perception of pain was completely fogged. The whole event couldn't have taken more than ten seconds from start to finish. I do know that when I stood up, I had complete presence of mind while lines of blood streamed down my face. I had no idea how badly I had been hurt, but I knew the one thing that mattered most: my legs worked. That meant I had a shot to hike out. Tim and I immediately moved to a shaded spot about fifty yards up the trail from the attack site and he began to do triage on my injuries. Tim feared the bear would return, but I knew that was unlikely. The encounter with two humans that resulted in a snootful of bear spray had been as traumatic for the grizzly as it was for us. That bear was long gone.

Training in first aid is an absolute must if you're going to venture into the backcountry, so I dumped the contents of my first aid kit on the ground and instructed Tim on what to do.

The greatest immediate concern seemed to be my head; now he could see that the young bruin had torn a gaping, four-inch-long, inch-wide wound in my scalp from the back of my head to the front. As Tim poured hydrogen peroxide on my head to prevent infection, my mind slipped into survival mode. I experienced perfect clarity and speed of thought. I knew exactly where I was, exactly the hike that lay ahead, the difficulty of the terrain, everything. Most of all, I knew I didn't want to be left in the backcountry. I was bound and determined to get my ass out of there on my own if I could.

Tim used gauze and a torn T-shirt to create a sort of turban on my head, bandaged my wounded left wrist with gauze, then went back for my camera and snapped a few pictures of the scene for documentation. In the back of my mind, I was concerned about the welfare of the bear. I knew that due to the public's fascination with animal attacks (and particularly with grizzly bears), if word got out, the media would be all over us at the hospital. I was certain this had been a spontaneous, surprise-driven attack, and I didn't want the bear to pay the price because of public alarm that could create a witch-hunt atmosphere. Because I was familiar with Park Service policy—they would not take action if a bear attack was considered a surprise, defensive encounter—I was confident that under these circumstances the bear would not be pursued.

After rendering first aid, Tim took the heaviest items from my pack, including the camera gear, and put them in his own, easily shouldering more than fifty pounds. It was 3:30 P.M. We were ten-and-a-half miles from the car. It was a long way to go with serious injuries, even for someone in my kind of shape. But spending the night was not an option. My adrenaline was pumping hard and I knew what I had to do. I knew my legs were unscathed, but I couldn't possibly know the extent of my other injuries, and did not focus on them. I knew it was important that I take advantage of my initial surge of energy to put as many miles behind me as possible. We left some of our trash out so rangers could find the spot for their investigation, and prepared to head back up Flattop Mountain.

Tim hung behind to get organized, but I aggressively set out and was chewing up the trail as fast as I could go. Of course, it helped that I had a light pack; Tim was the one who would be trying to keep up while lugging a big load. After a while I was three or four miles up the trail, charged up and eager to get to safety. I felt wired after my encounter with the great bear, not only in the "I've just survived a brush with death" way, but also in a primal way.

It was a stroke of luck that we were at the steepest uphill portion of the trail, because that was when I had the most energy from my adrenaline rush. I knew I needed to get that uphill stretch behind me while I could still handle it. If I had been forced to hike that steep section at the end, it would have been far more formidable, and I don't know what would have happened.

As I was barreling downhill through the meadows, I reached back to wipe what I assumed was sweat off the back of my neck and my hand came back bright red. I momentarily thought, "This is serious," but didn't break my stride. The odds of running into someone on the trail this time of year were remote, so Tim and I had to assume we were on our own.

It was likely a combination of blood loss, fatigue, low blood sugar, and the easing of my adrenaline surge, but my energy was beginning to run low. I stopped and waited for Tim, and when he caught up with me, I informed him I no longer had the strength to carry a pack. So poor Tim lashed my pack to his with rope and set out with miles to go carrying a crippling eighty pounds on his back.

We trudged on, and with about four miles to go, we entered the switchbacks through the thick timber. This worried me. Up to now, the landscape had been open to the sky, so a rescue helicopter would have been able to see me and land nearby. No more. In the trees there was no way a chopper could land. This was my point of no return. By entering this area, I had made a conscious commitment to making it to safety on my own, because I was putting myself effectively beyond the reach of any immediate help. The other thing I was thinking about was my sister arriving and the possible media coverage of the attack depending on how quickly the press got wind of it. What would she think if she ran across a secondhand or sensationalized version of the story before she arrived? More important, what would she think when she saw me? All this was running through my mind for four hours during the grueling hike out.

Then, with about three miles left, I ran out of gas. Just ran out. I simply could not walk another step. My body was slightly chilled by my blood-soaked T-shirt. Tim caught up to me and we sat by the trail trying to figure out our next move, and the upside and downside of him leaving to get help. The gravity of the situation had reached a different level, because a rescue would probably not have come until morning, and I didn't relish the idea of spending the night out in the wilderness alone. I wasn't worried about the cold; the nights were still relatively mild and I had warm clothing in my pack. But I didn't know if I would have the strength to make a fire, and worst of all, I would be alone and largely defenseless in the wild, reeking of blood. That potent smell could attract predators, including another grizzly bear. If I had been forced to spend the night, I would have set up camp in a place that was as safe as possible, with my back to a large tree or rocks, and tried to stay awake all night.

I think the key was that I was in a survival mindset and stayed as positive as possible. Tim and I were talking over our options when good old common sense reasserted itself—and we realized we hadn't had anything to eat or drink since lunch hours before. "How stupid," I thought. "You've had this happen, you've lost blood, and you haven't put anything back into your body." We pulled water and protein bars from our packs and I inhaled them. A surge of energy flowed back into my body, giving me a second wind. I could now forge ahead, which was a huge relief.

The elation was short-lived, however, because there was plenty of work ahead of me. I realized that I was having more trouble with the short uphill stretches on the trail than I had ever had before. Hardly surprising, but still, I had never noticed the difference between up and down as much as at that time.

We finally reached Mineral Creek, and as I sat down to remove my boots and wade across, Tim accidentally leaned on his bear spray, which was aimed directly at my face with the safety disengaged. Thankfully, there was almost no spray left, and after the attack I had just survived, a little sting in the eyes was child's play. I pointed out to Tim that he had now sprayed a bear and a person in the same day; we laughed about it and that lightened the mood.

So it was in relatively good shape and good humor that we reached the trailhead and the glorious sight of our car. This was like a piano being lifted off my back. I still didn't feel any pain, and I wasn't even particularly concerned at that point. I knew my injuries were not life threatening; after all, I had just walked more than ten miles in this condition. But I was beginning to feel tired. We slid into the car just before dark and sped off to the village of West Glacier. There Tim stopped to call the hospital from a pay phone and we had a curiously fortuitous encounter. A gentleman was at another pay phone close to Tim, overheard the conversation, came over and introduced himself as a physician and offered to assess my condition. Who says the pay phone is obsolete?

After my first book, *Lives of Grizzlies: Montana and Wyoming*, came out in 2004, I received a letter from Dr. John Herbst with his recounting of the story. Up to that point in time, after over eleven years, I never knew the identity of the mystery doctor. Now I can let Dr. Herbst fill in the blanks with a letter he wrote to me, dated December 18, 2004:

In late September 1993 I was on a photography trip to my favorite place in the world, Glacier National Park. On the evening of September 29th, after a wonderful day in the park, I was checking in with my family back home on a pay phone in West Glacier.

As I was speaking with my family, a vehicle roared up, a gentleman exploded out of the vehicle, ran up and started speaking on the pay phone next to me. In a most excited and concerned voice, he explained to whomever was on the other end of the phone that his friend had been mauled by a grizzly "while hiking up by Fifty Mountain" and that they were on their way to the hospital in Kalispell. I, being a doctor, immediately hung up the phone and offered my assistance.

I found a bloody gentleman with a gauze turban that was caked in blood sitting in the passenger side of the vehicle. The gentleman who had been mauled was remarkably calm and coherent. I explained that I was a physician and checked to make sure that the mauling victim was stable . . . he was breathing well; did not appear to be in hemodynamic shock; had no apparent serious spinal, chest, or abdominal injuries; had surprisingly low pulse and respiratory rates for what he had experienced and all bleeding seem to have stopped. He did appear to have an injury to his hand but in short, I saw no immediately life-threatening injuries.

I commended the non-injured companion on his care of the

victim and offered to accompany the two gentlemen to Kalispell. The non-injured gentleman thanked me for my attention to his friend and stated he felt they could make it to the hospital in good shape . . . subsequently, he jumped into the vehicle and drove rapidly out of West Glacier and turned towards Kalispell on Highway 2.

The next day, I called the hospital in Kalispell to try and see how this victim had faired but could not get any information. I went to the hospital to check on the victim but was not allowed to make contact. I called my acquaintance in the park, Amy Vanderbilt, who told me the mauling victim was doing well. I did manage to see an article in the newspaper about the incident and it sounded like the injured person would make a good recovery.

I have had a life-long fascination with grizzly bears and have spent many hours observing them in Glacier Park. There has been a recurring theme in my life of grizzly bear encounters that I have had in the park that subsequently came back "full circle" at a later time . . . sometimes with almost mystical ramifications. With this in mind, while visiting our local Borders bookstore here in Rapid City, South Dakota, I could not help but pick up and immediately purchase a book that I saw entitled *Lives of Grizzlies: Montana and Wyoming* by Jim Cole.

Last evening I was reading the section on Glacier Park with great fascination as the words and photographs jogged many memories of my times with bears in Glacier Park. I was just about ready to put the book down and head for bed when I began reading a section with the subheading "My Closest Encounter." As I read this section, something seemed vaguely familiar about the story. As I read on and got to page 95 where I read the words "Coincidentally, a doctor was using the adjoining phone," I was stunned and felt goose bumps arise as did the hair on the back of my neck. I had to have been that doctor.

I am so glad you made a good recovery from your encounter and I thank you for your wonderful new book. I wish you and your loved ones a most happy and healthy Holiday Season.

Thank you, Dr. Herbst. You were a welcome encounter.

Upon my arrival at Kalispell Regional Hospital near Glacier Park, I was awake, lucid, and not very happy to see a local TV reporter approach the car. Word of maulings travels quickly in this part of the world. I didn't want to be photographed in this condition; publicizing my injuries would only create undue alarm and increase irrational fear of the great bear. Tim told the reporter to give me a wide berth and he complied. After I was inside, Tim gave an interview that kept the press off my back.

All things considered, I wasn't in too bad shape when I walked into the Kalispell trauma center. I had a broken hand and a ghastly scalp wound that needed to be stapled back together, but all in all, not bad for my first bear attack. The staff, as Dr. Herbst had been, was surprised at how calm I was. But I had spent years around these great animals, and I knew what happened had not been the act of some sort of evil, man-eating beast. It had been a fluke, one part of the totality of the grizzly wilderness experience.

Later, a Park Service ranger came to see me during my

hospital stay and interviewed me about the attack. I knew that park policy was to give the bears the benefit of the doubt, so I wasn't surprised when the rangers investigated the scene and decided that the attack had been a surprise, defensive encounter. That was good medicine for my spirits—unless you were my doctors and nurses, who wanted me to spend more time in the hospital. But I had my family coming to town and I wasn't going to greet them from a hospital bed if I had anything to say in the matter. Reluctantly, the hospital set me up with a fanny pack containing a programmed IV that would pump antibiotics into my system to counteract the virulent bacteria that can be in a bear's mouth.

Thus attired, I had Tim drive me to Kalispell airport the day after the attack to pick up my sister, brother-in-law, and Molly. Molly is an experienced nurse who could look after me when I was away from the hospital, and it was this tidbit that had helped sell my doctors on letting me go so soon.

We arrived ten minutes late, and let me explain what that means in my family. We were raised in a home where punctuality was next to godliness; unless you were bleeding from the head or neck, you were simply on time for things. So when my sister had picked up her luggage and I still wasn't there, she knew something was wrong. Finally, up I strolled in my turban and sling, and at first they thought the whole thing was a gag. I can be a clown, but when they saw the wounds and the antibiotic pump, they knew I had taken quite a detour on the way to the airport. They spent the first few days of their stay at my West Glacier cabin, nursing me back to health.

There's an interesting epilogue to this story. Shortly after the attack, we got word that our father was scheduled to go in for his second quadruple bypass surgery, so my sister and I decided that I would go back to Chicago with her to be with Dad. I hadn't told my father about the attack because I didn't want it to be on his mind, but when he came to pick us up at O'Hare and saw me, he was shocked and concerned. But he remained every inch the dad: two weeks before his surgery, he took me to a White Sox playoff game and as we were walking to our seats, he was protecting me, making sure I walked with my right side, not my injured side, exposed to the jostling of other fans, and making sure no one bumped into me. It touched me then and touches me now. Then, after his surgery, we switched roles and I took care of him.

While I was in Chicago recovering and helping look after Dad, I stayed at my sister's house in Deerfield, near where I grew up. She had a bird feeder in back, and my favorite bird has always been the red cardinal. One morning, I saw one sitting on a branch near the feeder, got my camera out of the holster to take a shot of it . . . and saw that the viewfinder mirror was cracked and there was the huge indentation of a canine tooth mark in the body. I realized for the first time that the grizzly had actually bitten into my side, not just torn away the camera holster. But instead of getting a mouthful of Jim, it had gotten a mouthful of camera and holster and let go. The camera had protected me from a far more serious injury to my side that would have surely kept me from hiking out. A severe wound, a night alone in the wild—who knows, that camera may have saved my life.

So I was lucky. And as soon as my wrist healed, I got back into grizzly country. As I've said, the only changes I made were carrying two cans of bear spray and making more noise as I hiked. Other than that, I was back out on the trails as usual the following spring. I was ecstatic. I felt confident. I figured I had survived a grizzly bear attack and hiked out under my own power. That had to be the worst Nature could ever throw at me, right?

2

The Misunderstood Monarch

With logging and mining, so many new roads
For the lowly bear there's no place to go
With habitat shrinking, that's not what they need
Stuck at the mercy of money and greed
When a hunter approaches, they'd best say a prayer
'Cause life isn't fair, when you're a bear
Life isn't fair when you're a bear

—"Life Isn't Fair When You're a Bear," music and lyrics by James R. Cole

REMEMBER A MOVIE FROM a few years back called *The Edge*, which starred Anthony Hopkins and Alec Baldwin as two rivals for the same woman stranded in the wilderness and pursued by an enraged brown bear? That would never happen in the real world. *Ever.* As far as we know, the only creatures to hold grudges are humans; bears don't indulge in vendettas. Like most wild animals, they avoid contact with us whenever possible. If they are surprised, feel threatened, or are tempted by food, they can attack people with a ferocity and power that are hard to believe, but only for as long as they perceive the threat to exist. Once the threat is gone or they have their food, they usually vanish. The idea of a grizzly pursuing Oscar-winning actors through the wilds of the north is, to put it mildly, ridiculous. Sit back while I tell you another kind of bear story.

The unmistakable sound of an approaching animal crackling through fallen leaves woke me at 3 A.M. at my campsite in the rugged Alaska wilderness. I crawled half-naked out of my tent as a big grizzly slowly but deliberately walked toward me. I didn't see any aggression in its behavior, just wary curiosity. The bear stopped within ten feet of me as we both stood motionless, staring at each other in the moonlit silence. The moon was only two-thirds full, but on this crystal clear autumn night the woods were lit up and alive, illuminating the outline of every branch and trunk. Time stood still; the moment was surreal but I never felt fearful or threatened. The peaceful bruin looked into my eyes and sniffed the air as we both remained still. After about a minute, the bear calmly turned and walked away, making a slow noisy exit through the piles of brittle windblown autumn leaves. As the crunching steps faded into the forest, I settled back into my sleeping bag. I was unbelievably exhilarated as I lay awake for the next couple of hours still visualizing this wilderness monarch, who had made quiet peace with a defenseless human being in the middle of its kingdom.

That's the grizzly bear that I know: intelligent, inquisitive, majestic, calm, and in complete command of its domain. The grizzly is the lord of its ecosystem; the only creature that poses a threat to it (other than another bear) is man. Bears actually tolerate the presence of you and me quite well, something proven by the fact that millions of visitors travel through Yellowstone each year to watch grizzlies—including mothers with cubs—as they sometimes cross park roads and wander among cars while foraging for food, without anyone getting hurt or even feeling threatened. In fact, bears in some areas are more comfortable around humans than I would like. Generally speaking, a grizzly that avoids human contact stands a far better chance of living a long, healthy life than one that feels comfortable around roads, campsites, and other human development.

Human beings have been awed by the grizzly bear's size and power for millennia. Among the Native American nations such as the Sioux, who occupied the Great Plains for many centuries before the arrival of the white man, only the bison rivaled the great bruin as an icon of might and grandeur. The bear was sacred, a kindred spirit to the native tribes. On the rare occasions when they hunted the bear, Native Americans did so with respect and humility, and used every part of the animal. Hunting the grizzly before the introduction of firearms usually meant tracking the bear to its den in the autumn, then returning to attack in winter when the bruin was most vulnerable. If you surprised a grizzly armed only with a bow and arrow or a knife, you had better be right with the Great Spirit or be very, very skillful or lucky.

Grizzlies are a species distinct from the smaller and far

more common North American black bear. Forget about the colors as identifiers, however; either species can be black, brown, blond, or a range of colors in between. What sets the grizzly apart is its characteristic shoulder hump, a concave facial profile, its famously long claws (tailor-made for digging out worms, roots, insects, and rodents), and its size. The grizzly's northern cousins, the coastal brown bears (including the Kodiak bear of Alaska and the peninsular brown bear of Russia), can grow to 1,500 pounds on their rich diet of salmon, salmon, and more salmon. Imagine a locomotive with fur and you have the idea. In contrast, inland grizzlies like those in Montana and Wyoming rely more on berries, white bark pine nuts, grubs, moths, and roots than on meat for their calories (though Yellowstone bears are more meat-reliant than other interior bears), so adults are more likely to weigh 300 to 500 pounds, typically topping out at perhaps 800 pounds. But that's still quite a lot of bear.

Grizzlies are bristling with contradictions. Many folks see their size and lumbering gait and assume they're slow, clumsy, and stupid. Hardly. On flat ground, a grizzly can run up to thirty-five miles an hour, which is why if you get on a bear's bad side, outdistancing it is really not an option. They are also very agile and light on their feet; I have seen them jump creeks, seamlessly squeeze under logs, and chase down elk calves with a grace that was almost balletic. Also, the bears are extremely intelligent (animal behaviorists rank them somewhere between a smart dog and an ape) and learn quickly, which is why it's so vital when camping in the backcountry to secure your food either in bear-proof containers or tied be-tween trees. All breeds of bears are ingenious at figuring out ways to pilfer stores of beef jerky, trail mix, and peanut butter, and though adult grizzlies are generally not adept climbers, if there's a way to get your supplies, they'll probably find it.

One aspect of the grizzly that I find most captivating is its face. The grizzly doesn't look at you with the wary stalker's face you would expect from a predator like a mountain lion or wolf. Its small ears are propped on top of its head looking for all the world like the ears of the stuffed bear you slept with when you were six. Its intense eyes are close-set around its muzzle, surrounded by that dish-shaped, round, furry face, and it stares at you with such candid curiosity and intelligence that it's utterly disarming. What a noble face, the face of a monarch who fears nothing within his domain. It doesn't al-ways look like an animal that belongs at the top of the food chain. With its ample hindquarters and a kind of bemused expression, it looks like it should be grabbing a lunch bucket, hitching up its pants, and heading off to work as a city bus driver—Jackie Gleason in *The Honeymooners*.

That endearing, gentle quality is why I feel such frustra-tion at the common public perception that the bears are vi-cious killing machines whose shadow should make you quake with terror every time you venture into the wild country. Now, let's be realistic: grizzly bears are awesomely powerful animals, and under the right (or wrong) conditions, they are nearly unstoppable predators. Their jaws generate one of the most powerful bites in nature and their claws can be four inches long or longer, driven by muscles that can (and do) rip open the tops of steel trash bins like they're made of aluminum foil. You should respect their power whenever you go into their territory, but that's especially true whenever you lace up a pair of hiking boots and hoist a backpack to head into the wilderness.

Make no mistake, if that bear had come upon my camp in Alaska with the intent to kill and eat me, he could have. There would have been virtually nothing I could have done to stop him. Yet you're far more likely to die of drowning, hypothermia, a bad fall, or a heart attack out in the wild than you are to be killed by grizzly. If you understand the essentials about grizzly behavior and respect their beauty and power, then you'll go into the backcountry prepared and knowledgeable about how to behave . . . without the need for fear.

Unless you're a young elk calf or an injured ungulate (a bison, deer, moose, elk, or caribou), the odds that you will be attacked by a grizzly in the wild, even if you see one a short distance away, are astronomical. So why do people have such a knee-jerk fear of the great bear, as I did when I saw my first black bear at Camp Menominee? It's largely a media fabrication that reflects both the modern human's separation from and fear of the wilderness and the news machine's fascination with stories of gore and man-versus-beast survival like *Untamed and Uncut* or *When Animals Attack*. Remember, one of my concerns after my 1993 attack was that once the media got hold of it, the story would be turned into a sensationalist rant about the dangers of the grizzly. That kind of fear tends to be justified because of the media's "if it bleeds, it leads" policy. But as we will see, the fear and sensationalism are just not supported by the facts.

There is no question that grizzly bears are potentially dangerous wild animals that can and will kill humans. But it is a very rare day when a bear does attack a human, especially considering the number of people who annually recreate in grizzly country.

Despite my misfortunes, I still firmly believe that the risk is minimal. It is important to understand that grizzly attacks are almost never predatory. If a habituated bear views areas of human activity—trash disposal areas, campsites, or picnic grounds—as potential food sources, then it might brave human proximity in order to get at some tasty morsels. But otherwise, bears generally want nothing to do with humans. They know that humans mean danger. Like any wild animal, the most common response when a grizzly encounters a human is flight. The reason two encounters of mine resulted in maulings was because I surprised the bears and they felt they had no other options.

I have never had a problem with a bear when I spotted the bear before the bear detected me, or when the bear was made aware of my presence (either through scent or noise) with enough time to put a safe distance between us. My two attacks would almost certainly never have occurred if I had seen the bear first, had a few seconds to back away to a distance that did not pose a threat to the animals, and had time to pull out my bear spray. In virtually every other surprise meeting I have ever had at close range with a non-habituated grizzly, the bruin instantly dashed away to what it perceived as a safer area.

When I camped on the shore of a remote lake in the Kodiak National Wildlife Refuge in July 2001, all I saw from the bears in this salmon-rich ecosystem was submissive behavior—resulting in avoidance, retreat, and fear—when they detected my presence. To quote from my book, *Lives of Grizzlies: Alaska:*

For the first two days I hiked several miles up and down the creek, mostly through dense foliage on the bluffs. While thrashing along I spooked several bears from their daybeds. When bears became aware of me near the creek, they always made a quick exit. No bear was ever threatening. Every bruin that saw, heard, or smelled me immediately took off. With the wind blowing hard at my back, I watched through binoculars as a female with cubs picked up my scent from over a half-mile away. Her nose was sniffing in my direction before she made a hasty retreat. These were wary bears that rarely saw people. No other humans were staying in this area, and I later learned that I may have been the only person to camp here in several years. My strategy had to change. I could not continue to disturb and displace bears.

Approximately three million human visitors annually enter Yellowstone Park in motorized vehicles. Each person, couple, family, or group enters this national wilderness sanctuary with various expectations, backgrounds, life experiences, personal interests, passions, and plans. The Grand Loop Road, shaped like a figure eight with five distinct branches exiting the park to the north, south, east, west, and northwest, showcases striking scenery and varied natural features as it winds through the heart of Yellowstone. All in all, the 310-mile, well-maintained paved road system offers visitors a whole lot to see without wandering very far from the car.

Despite this, human fatalities occur virtually every year in Yellowstone Park from various causes, but the vast majority of these tragic incidents do not involve any wild animals. *Death in Yellowstone,* a 1995 book written by Lee H. Whittlesey, is the most reliable source on this morbid subject. The topic of death in the park becomes particularly important in the examination of the relative risks a person takes when they voluntarily enter the boundaries of our oldest national park.

According to this book, the total number of violent deaths that occurred in Yellowstone between 1839 and 1993 is over 300, not including automobile and snowmobile accidents. Whittlesey talks about the most common causes of visitor fatalities in the park, and the results may surprise you.

Drowning is number one. More than one hundred visitors have drowned in Yellowstone, presumably (though this is speculation on my part) from activities like slipping and falling while trying to cross rivers or tiring and developing hypothermia while swimming in lakes.

As of 1995, there had been at least twenty-four deaths in the park from falls, the second most common cause of fatalities. Most of the falls have occurred when visitors hiking in the backcountry got too close to a steep drop in order to take in a spectacular view.

The number-three cause of death has been from visitors falling into thermal features, such as boiling hot springs. Nineteen people perished this way through 1995, says Whittlesey. They include young children who got away from their parents, teens who were walking on the thin surface of a feature where they didn't belong, fisherman who accidentally stepped into hot springs near Yellowstone Lake, and park employees taking illegal swims in thermal pools. Sixteen more park visitors have been hospitalized over the last ten years due to burns from geysers or hot springs.

The fourth most common cause of fatality is avalanche. There have been six avalanche fatalities in Yellowstone. One of them was my friend Greg Felzein, who died tracking a radio-collared male mountain lion on February 22, 1992. We were working together on a mountain lion study conducted by the Wildlife Research Institute, which was headquartered at the University of Idaho. A couple of nights earlier, I was teaching him how to play the banjo at the Wapiti Bar in the town of Gardiner. Greg was as competent as anybody in the backcountry and enjoyed working alone. Everyone on the project was often required to work solo and had to be confident in their wilderness survival skills. The avalanche that killed Greg was one hundred yards long, ten yards wide, and five feet deep. Seven rescue workers, including his best friend,

Todd Frederickson, who also worked on the study, found his body face down, not completely covered with snow.

According to Whittlesey, the other causes of death in Yellowstone are lightning strikes (at least five deaths during the park's history), falling trees (four, maybe five, fatalities), rockslides (three or perhaps four deaths), and consumption of the poisonous water hemlock (two known deaths), one of only two plants in the park dangerous enough to kill a human.

There have been two confirmed human deaths from bison in Yellowstone. I suspect that in great part this is because inexperienced visitors don't perceive the big, shaggy, apparently slow-moving ungulates as a threat—at least, not compared with the dramatic jaws and claws of a 350-pound grizzly. But there is a reason that the one animal in the Yellowstone ecosystem that even a big adult male bear won't mess with is a full-grown bison: they are 2,000 pounds of hooves and horns that can run up to thirty-five miles an hour. A bison may look harmless, but it is the most powerful animal in Yellowstone and if harassed or threatened can be extremely dangerous. Yet the average person is likely to fear the secretive and shy grizzly more than the more common bison.

Michael Milstein in an article for the *Gazette Wyoming Bureau,* updated April 18, 2000, notes:

Shaggy bison may not conjure up the same kind of fearsome campfire tales as grizzly bears, but they have charged, butted, or gored twice as many YNP visitors than grizzly bears have injured in the last two decades, a new study shows.

Bison have charged people eighty-one times since 1978, according to a listing of park conflicts between people and wildlife other than bears compiled by Jim and Edna Caslick. The bison made contact with the person in each case, but not all of the people were seriously injured.

Park visitors died from bison related injuries in 1984 and 1991. In contrast, grizzly bears have killed two since 1978.

"We've always known that bison hurt more people than bears, but I didn't know they hurt as many more people as they do," said park biologist Tom Oliff, who oversaw the study.

The high toll may be due to the public perception of bison, biologists said. While most people respect or even fear bears, many do not think of shaggy and lumbering bison as dangerous. Oliff pointed out that, "People don't understand that bison can be dangerous. They don't look dangerous, but they are amazingly quick and amazingly agile when they want to be."

All of the bison charges appeared to be defensive reactions to people who approached them too closely. A few of the charges may have been triggered when people walked up on bison without realizing it.

Yet we don't hear a call to arms sounding against Bison Nation, do we? When someone tells a friend that he's going to hike in bison country, the reaction is usually a shrug, rather than the "Are you crazy?" that comes if the hiker announces he's camping in grizzly territory. It's all a matter of perspective.

However, the above statistics should never give park visitors cause to be complacent or let their guard down with respect to grizzly bears or any of the potential dangers that Yellowstone presents. There is no substitute for knowledge and plain old common sense.

Human beings have a visceral fascination with big, dangerous, enigmatic predators—sharks, crocodiles, big cats, and grizzly bears. When someone talks about a bear attack, the eyes of inexperienced outdoorsmen grow wide and they start seeing bears everywhere. I think this stems in part from lack of understanding of the odds of even seeing a bear, and also from the idea that when you're in the bear's realm, you give up control. There's something out there that's bigger, faster, and far more powerful than you are. That unsettling idea freaks some people out. It's the same kind of irrational fear that makes some afraid of flying when driving is statistically much more hazardous.

A friend of mine has an odd perspective I honestly don't understand. He believes that my educational elementary school grizzly bear programs are doing a disservice to children by teaching them not to fear grizzly bears. Though he has never seen a wild grizzly, he firmly believes that these creatures are not predictable and that "people have to have a healthy fear." I think a little bit of healthy fear is beneficial, but nothing I have said has ever diminished his apprehension. In his view, many visitors consider Yellowstone Park a big zoo and they "think they are being protected in this closed environment by park rangers." I think the only way to give these animals a chance for survival is to understand them—and our fear of them—by learning the facts.

Black bears are relatively common, with between 75,000 and 100,000 estimated to live in at least thirty-two of the lower forty-eight states, and tend to be much more adaptable to living near humans. Grizzlies, which require a much larger habitat area and tend to avoid human contact, number only about 1,100 in the contiguous states, occupying approximately 2 percent of their historical range. So the odds that you will encounter a grizzly are slim to none, especially if you're taking care to make plenty of noise as you hike and to keep your food out of reach when you camp. But even if you see a grizzly, a bad outcome is very unlikely.

These are the blue collar, beer league softball players of the animal kingdom: loving, playful, and curious. Mother bears are strict but devoted parents, cautious and observant around humans, and driven by a sense of smell that's about one hundred times keener than yours and mine. They are loners, something I have in common with them. And they are always hungry (something I also have in common with them), driven by a constant need to pack on body fat to see them through winter hibernation, when some bears will shed up to 25 percent of their body weight. When food becomes scarce in one area due to drought, development, or competition from other bears, grizzlies will sometimes roam great distances to find food, which can include moths, ants, carrion, and all kinds of berries—as well as human trash, which has become the crack cocaine of the bear world and the cause of so many bear-human problems.

More than three decades in the field have proven to me that individual grizzlies have some predictable patterns of behavior. Once I get to know a bear, I can often anticipate what it will do, just as anyone can with a person that they know well. But if a strange bear comes into my yard, I have no idea what it will do. In general, these are overwhelmingly shy creatures whose main interest is to avoid uncomfortable human contact, which you can see when you observe bruins that wander near the main roads at parks like Yellowstone. When this occurs, the famous "bear jams" may follow: rangers manage the traffic and people on the road to let the bears forage and cross, and excited visitors hop out of their cars, cameras clicking away. Most grizzlies are uneasy with this situation; people worry them. Some will immediately leave the area if they see humans, while others will pace and observe warily, sometimes dragging a carcass out of sight of humans before feeding.

Let me take a second to differentiate between *human-habituated* and *food-conditioned* bears. Human-habituated bears are accustomed to varying degrees of human presence in their territory and will tolerate people standing nearby, quietly observing or taking pictures as they forage. Bears that are habituated to humans (usually mothers with cubs or young bears, almost never solitary adult males) will sometimes purposefully seek out roadside habitats for a good reason: they have become comfortable around humans because they know that other bears are uneasy around us and will avoid the area, freeing them to forage and feed without worrying about competition and danger. In some cases, it may take only a lone human in the backcountry to give human-tolerant, subordinate bears security during a feeding opportunity.

For example, a mother grizzly and her yearling cub warily fed on a dead bison during a glorious early morning in the northern reaches of Hayden Valley near Alum Creek in Yellowstone. I stood out in the open about a hundred yards away as the mom kept her eye on me but obviously did not perceive my presence as a threat. In fact, just the opposite. I believe she welcomed my human stench. Two lone grizzlies, one a formidable male, were circling the scene but would not approach because I stood nearby. Since I never wear camouflage, my figure was easily visible and with very little wind, they surely caught my scent.

With abundant protein calories at hand, the bear family gorged because my presence kept the two wary bears from approaching. The two intruders wanted no part of me and drifted away without incident as mother and cub filled their bellies. I stood motionless in the same spot, observed and photographed for nearly two hours and, as the bear mom periodically looked my way, it seemed that she was thanking me. Without my inadvertent help, the bear family would likely be foraging through the relatively meager sagebrush vegetation and digging up pocket gopher caches.

Food-conditioned bears, however, are another matter. They are problem bears. Not only have they lost their fear of humans but they have developed a taste for (or a dependence on) human food. They are the bears that make forays into villages, break into trash barrels, invade campsites, and consume food either accepted directly from humans or found along roadsides. Despite ample warnings and strict laws, human feeding of bears remains a shrinking but still serious, persistent problem. A minority of ignorant visitors continue to do it because the bears "look so cute," never understanding that they are endangering the animals' survival. The many possible negatives of a human-bear encounter (which usually involve someone overreacting or doing something stupid and the bear being blamed) often lead rangers to move carrion away from roads so that bears can feed at a safe distance from *homo sapiens*.

Let me be clear: the grizzly bear is not enigmatic. With rare exceptions, the only time you may be in any danger from a grizzly is if you make the animal feel threatened with your actions and noises or by surprising it, especially if it's a mother with cubs. Otherwise, the great bears are quite tolerant of us . . . probably more tolerant than we deserve and certainly more tolerant than we are of them.

Even when you have observed grizzlies for as long as I have, they can still do things that leave you awed and humbled. A few years back, I was casually watching a family of bears near a lake in the early afternoon as the mother bear approached along the beach with three small spring cubs trailing close behind in single file. I calmly stayed motionless as she stopped less than thirty yards away to check me out (though we already knew each other) and survey the scene for threats. She sat and looked around for about twenty minutes as the cubs napped behind her in the sand. When she seemed satisfied that the coast was clear, she brought the cubs even closer then took a sharp right turn into the lake, leaving her brood with me.

Let me reiterate that: *a mother grizzly had left her cubs with me*, essentially as a kind of babysitter. As a first-time mom, she adhered to an ultra-cautious strategy to keep her cubs safe from other bears, but with humans, based on the way she behaved around me, she danced to a different tune. I knew that her behavior and trust of me had been learned from her incredible mother, who still patrolled this same home range with two new cubs and who five years earlier had approached me and done the same thing with her cubs. Mother had taught daughter to trust certain humans . . . and I was deeply honored to be one of them.

For over half an hour, Mama Bear kept a periodic eye on all of us as she caught and consumed several red salmon more than one hundred yards out in the frigid lake. Then another bear approached her, and she frantically huffed and plunged her way through the water toward her helpless offspring, who were nervously waiting near me along the beach. When the dripping wet mother bear arrived on shore, she continued to look back at the intruding bear, who was just innocently fishing, as the three nervous whining cubs gathered at her feet. At that salmon-filled lake, many of the bears were familiar with each other and knew who posed a threat. But when push comes to shove, a mother grizzly takes no chances with her cubs.

After several more purposeful glances out into the lake, the mother bear slowly walked toward me in a submissive posture. The bear family wasn't far away as she abruptly rolled over onto her back for a nursing session that would both feed and calm her cubs. Amazed at this, I respectfully watched and photographed. She seemed to feel both safe and extremely comfortable in this spot, while the cubs purred loudly as they sucked in the rich liquid nourishment from their mother's body. It was clear she and I shared a mutual trust that I could never put into words—and which I would never violate.

Having spent so much time in grizzly country, I have had many other moments that rivaled this one—moments that leave me dumbstruck with gratitude. But irrational fears persist in others, and the primary reason people feel imperiled by the bear—and the main reason the bear itself is threatened with extinction—is because we and they are forced to coexist at such close range. Grizzlies need a lot of room to roam, which is why modern human development of lands in the plains and foothills has proved so devastating to their numbers. A grizzly bear can range over a wide area, from mountaintops to alpine meadows to river bottoms, constantly searching for food. As you can imagine, even in the supposedly wide-open West, undeveloped, unspoiled wilderness is becoming hard to come by. Some humans have chosen to be adversaries to the great bear rather than partners, though we have the ability to coexist if we are willing to make some forward-thinking adaptations to how we live in bear country. Up to now, man has not shown that kind of vision. Hence the bears' reliance on protected areas like Glacier and Yellowstone—and the tragic number of bear casualties that can occur when grizzlies come into contact with unprepared and fearful humans outside park boundaries.

As omnivores that will eat anything from army cutworm moths to salmon to serviceberries, grizzlies favor a range with varied terrain. Because they are basically voracious appetites with legs, their habitat depends largely on where a reliable food source is available. When usual and favored seasonal food sources like huckleberries and elk and moose calves are not available, they'll readily move down the nutritional ladder to less calorie-rich meals like grasses, worms, herbs, tubers, and ants. Where you find food, you'll find grizzlies, which is unfortunately why they sometimes amble into human settlements and camps, their hyper-keen olfactory senses drawn by the whiff of cooked meat, discarded chip bags, candy bars, or just about anything else that's bad for them. This sense of smell is so strong that even a tube of lip balm left out at a campsite can attract a curious and hungry bruin. This is also why park officials forbid tourists from feeding the bears . . . but some do it anyway.

I've seen people who walked to within a few feet of an adult grizzly with a camera, trying for the perfect shot. I've also seen people throwing rocks and yelling at a bear from close range to get it to turn its head so they can get a better picture. John Hechtel, a biologist with the Alaska Department of Fish and Game, says that "Ninety-five percent of the time, people are responsible for determining whether the outcome of a bear encounter will be good or bad." That's true. These are not teddy bears. They're not even the more docile-looking bears you might see in a zoo. These are wild creatures and you are in their territory. Some of the horror stories you may have heard probably occurred for a simple reason: the people involved did not have the proper respect for the bears and their environment.

One unfortunate, tragic incident that has scarred the image of the grizzly was the death of bear enthusiast Timothy Treadwell and his girlfriend, Amie Huguenard, in 2003. I knew Timothy; he was as passionate about the great bruins as I am, but the biggest difference between us was that he lived among them for months at a time, year after year, in Katmai National Park in Alaska. He did that for thirteen summers until he was killed and eaten by one or more grizzlies. His work, life, and death were sensationalized and made famous by the 2005 Werner Herzog film *Grizzly Man*.

Timothy wasn't a neutral figure. Some people idolized him as someone living the natural harmony between man and beast. Others thought he was bordering on insane or had a death wish. I don't think either was true. I think he was simply someone like me who loved and had a deep passion for an incredible aspect of nature, but unlike me, he took his passion too close to the edge to give him much room for error. One of the cardinal rules in any venture into the wilderness is that you always try to create a margin that allows you to survive an adverse event. That's why I carry a first aid kit and emergency supplies and have maps so I can plan alternative routes in case of avalanche or flooding, and why I make noise in bear country.

Timothy Treadwell cut his margin down to a razor-thin sliver by living with the grizzlies and putting himself in a situation where he had no easy way out if things went bad. I think Timothy forgot that he was a human, and no matter how much time he spent with the bears, he was always going to be a stranger, an intruder, no matter how bearlike he became and no matter how much he yearned to be a bear. He also disdained bear spray for most of his years, he didn't use safety devices like electric fences, and he never, ever stored his food properly. In my opinion, he died in great part because he got cocky, ignored fundamental wisdom about surviving around the grizzly, and took chances that I would never take.

Even though no one really knows what happened, the theory is that he and Amie were killed not by one of the bears they lived with but by a rogue male that wandered into the area. We will never know for sure. The most notable aspect of his "expeditions" is that, despite his cavalier attitude, he was able to survive among the bears for thirteen years. This speaks volumes about the bears' tolerance and peace-loving nature. However, the only thing that matters to most people is that Timothy and Amie were killed and devoured by grizzly bears, and that lurid image further fans the flames of fear and misinformation.

That brings us to the subject of bear attacks and bear-related fatalities in Yellowstone. I think this column from Ben Long in the *High Country News*, sums up the all-too-common grizzly hysteria perfectly:

SPRING: TIME FOR THE NATIONAL PARK SERVICE TO CHILL OUT

Ah, spring: The blooms of flowers; the songs of birds; the paranoia from the National Park Service.

I have come to expect it as I expect the muddy boots at the door and crowded pews at Easter: If you live in the same states as Glacier or Yellowstone National Parks, you will hear the Annual Bear Report on the radio or newspapers, thanks to a government news release.

The chipper voice of the National Park Service official goes like this: "Just a friendly warning that the grizzly bears are emerging from their dens. Be extra careful when you visit your local national park." This year, my local park flack warned male bears would awaken "grumpy" and mother bears would "ferociously defend" their cubs.

First off, I have to wonder, this is news? Bears have emerged from their dens every year for tens of thousands of years. There is nothing particularly earth shattering about this. Of course the annual bear news release is newsworthy, simply because it involves bears and the press gobbles it up like a basket full of jelly beans. Why do grizzlies hog the press? How about spreading the love and giving black bears, marmots, ground squirrels, and other hibernators a moment in the spotlight?

Turns out, when it comes to natural hazards, bears are

pretty low on the list in western national parks. Bears just grab the headlines, the lip service, and the warning signs. Rangers would save more lives lecturing folks on lifejackets and issuing press releases about spring runoff. Better yet, they could remind motorists to slow down, as cars are much more deadly than grizzlies.

Perhaps park officials believe they are doing the bears a favor by warning hapless tourists that the animals are out and about. But I think they may be reinforcing an unintended—and counterproductive—message of bear-anoia.

The problem with incessantly warning people about bears is that it intends to inflate the perception of danger posed by wild animals and wilderness. We live in a world where people are increasingly afraid to explore nature or allow their kids to explore nature. I have seen park visitors literally refuse to leave their cars out of fears of bears, mountain lions, or other wildlife. When I finish laughing, it leaves me profoundly sad.

What is the real danger to humans from grizzlies in Yellowstone? Well, from 1980 to 1997, more than forty-seven million people visited Yellowstone National Park. During the same period, twenty-three people were injured by bears. This makes the chances of being injured by a bear in the park slightly more than one in two million. To put that in perspective, according to the National Weather Service, the odds of being struck by lightning in a given year are one in 700,000.

There have been five bear-caused human fatalities (and one other possible fatality) within Yellowstone National Park since it was founded. The possible fatality occurred in 1907 when a man was attacked by a female grizzly bear after he prodded her cub with an umbrella. However, the validity of this incident is questionable.

The first confirmed fatality occurred in 1916 when a grizzly bear killed a man in a roadside camp. The second occurred in August 1942, in the Old Faithful campground. The species of bear involved could not be determined. The third fatality occurred in June 1972, when a man returned at night to an illegal camp and approached to within fifty feet of a grizzly bear feeding on food that had been left out in the open. The fourth fatality occurred in July 1984, when a grizzly bear killed a backpacker in a backcountry campsite located on the southern end of White Lake. And in October 1986, the most recent fatality occurred when a photographer approached an adult female grizzly bear too closely in a meadow just north of Hayden Valley.

On a personal note, although I have absolutely no fear of bears, I do admit to some fear of bison. These huge ungulates are unpredictable and I find it almost impossible to differentiate between individual animals. I simply don't trust bison and always give them a wide berth. Nobody really knows what to do about an aggressive buffalo, which is basically an angry compact car that has a mind of its own. Here's a case in point:

It was early afternoon as my rollercoaster hike wound through a remote section of Hayden Valley. Just as my momentum crested at the top of a hill, I caught a brief glimpse of a big animal at point blank range. Though I had been making noise while treading my way through this tricky area, at first I thought it was a bear. Fortunately (so I initially thought) it was a lone male bison. But as I paused, the bull glared in my direction then started purposefully walking toward me. I pulled out my bear spray while spontaneously backpedaling in step with the bison, which continued its steady approach. As experienced as I am in the backcountry, I honestly didn't know what to do. This obviously wasn't a grizzly. Would bear spray work against a one-ton behemoth like this? Should I run? The animal seemed relentless but never stepped up his methodical pace.

As I backed down a knoll, I was momentarily out of the bison's field of vision. I sprinted about fifty yards at a ninety-degree angle away from the scene, then turned around to check on my pursuer. He was casually continuing his march in the original direction and never even glanced my way. The crisis was over. Was I ever in real danger? It beats the heck out of me.

Later that day, I told the story to my friend Kerry Murphy, a mountain lion biologist, and asked him what should I have done. Murph put his arms out, palms up, and shook his head sideways. Whenever I have asked other wildlife experts this question, a similar response always follows. Nobody really knows. It's no wonder that an intelligent, clear thinking grizzly bear would never consider challenging a healthy adult bison. They remain, even to most naturalists, a mystery wrapped in an enigma inside 2,000 pounds of muscle.

According to Kerry Gunther, Bear Management Office,

Yellowstone National Park, bear-caused human mortalities in the park have been few and far between within the past one hundred years. In three of the six cases I've cited, the offending bear seems to have been provoked by questionable human behavior. As of this writing, not one person has been killed by a bear in Yellowstone in more than twenty-three years, though I had to work awfully hard to keep that statistic intact.

A grizzly typically goes for the head and face when it attacks. If you can't use bear spray, the best defense (and the one I tried to use in my Glacier attack) is to fall to the ground, face-down with your legs spread to make it harder for the bear to flip you over, with your hands behind your head to protect your neck and spinal cord. Most wildlife experts advise people to play dead in a grizzly attack, the theory being that if the animal thinks you are no longer a threat, it will leave you alone. Struggling or fighting back usually ensures that the attack will continue and intensify, and it's no good anyway unless you're very strong and skilled with a knife or machete. Still, some experts advise fighting back to protect yourself.

Your most important means of defense in bear country is always your brain. On a sunny July afternoon in Glacier Park, as I hiked just west of Red Rock Lake on the east side of the park, I heard the unmistakable rustling of an animal in the dense green underbrush below the trail. I stopped to check out the source. With the aid of binoculars, I saw the sunlit head of a beautiful grizzly with two small cubs looking in my direction. The bears resumed foraging as another hiker stopped to ask me what I was looking at. The situation seemed innocent enough as I pointed out the bears; the gentleman seemed composed and genuinely interested. He asked a few questions and I whispered answers as he stood behind me.

Without warning, the mother bear looked anxiously toward us and began huffing as her two offspring gathered at her feet. I had no clue what the source for her alarm was, but when I turned around, the guy who had been sharing this peaceful observation was sprinting away from me. He had apparently "freaked out" and the alert mother bear saw this sudden, quick movement as threatening. She instantly switched from a calm mode to red alert. That is a blatant case of disturbing and provoking an animal with stupidity. Fortunately, rather than choose an aggressive response, the bear mom turned and led her children away into the dense underbrush. Given the choice, grizzlies nearly always choose to avoid conflict in spite of outrageous human behavior fueled by a complete lack of common sense.

If you come upon a grizzly bear in the backcountry, it's obviously in your best interest to make sure the bear perceives you as unthreatening, so the first rules are just simple common sense:

1. Stop.
2. Be calm.
3. Evaluate the situation.
4. Keep your eyes on the bear, so you know where it is at all times.

What is the bear up to? Try not to stare in a threatening way; I have never seen a bear react based on eye contact or my facial expression, but it's wise not to risk any perceived antagonism. If you're too close, slowly back away and enjoy a rare observation at a safe distance, or if you're uncomfortable, simply leave the area. If the bear charges, don't run unless you're close to a surefire safe zone like a car or a cabin. If you're in the open, forget it. The bear is faster than you are, and running will only activate its predatory chase instinct. Remain calm and stay still. Most charges are bluffs. Take out your bear spray (something you should always have in bear country), and if the bear gets too close discharge your spray. If you don't have spray, as the bear closes in, you have to make a split-second decision about when you should go down into a fetal position. If the grizzly perceives that you're not a threat, it may abort the charge and retreat. But there are no guarantees; each bear is an individual and will behave differently.

This is an important point to make: there is no such thing as a "typical" grizzly. Yes, there are some fairly predictable behavior patterns, but even those are hardly set in stone. Bears are as individual as human beings, and each has its own unique personality, reactions, and attitude toward humans. This is why it's so essential to stay cool and keep your eyes on the bear if you can. You need to know how it is going to respond to you being in its territory. You can't rely on patterns or reports of "typical" grizzly behavior. There is no such thing.

By the way, don't even consider climbing a tree. It's one of the worst things you can do. The only time to consider this option would be if you have a ton of time to get high into a tree, but even then it's not a great idea. If you can climb a tree, a grizzly bear of decent size has the capability to find the same branches and follow you up. It's not common, but I've seen adult grizzly bears up in trees. The tree as safety is a myth.

In bygone days, the park service used to promote climbing a tree as one of the better ways to escape an aggressive grizzly bear, something I often argued with them about. As a case in point, during my second trip to Kodiak Island back in the summer of 1993, I was hiking across bluffs in a remote river drainage. As I looked down at this muddy river, a dark blob high up in a tree looked out of place and immediately drew my attention. I pulled out my binoculars and, lo and behold, a brown bear was perched up there like an oversized condor. The grizzly wasn't large by Kodiak standards but still looked to weigh about 300 pounds.

What could have driven that bear up a tree? It could have been anything from escaping a bigger bear, a nice view, or an afternoon siesta with a breeze. But the point is that even with a large body mass and long claws, grizzlies can climb trees. Cubs climb with ease and the bigger the bear, the less nimble it is at climbing. Big males would presumably have the most difficulty, but I assume nothing and very little surprises me about these animals.

It's safe to say that the relationship between grizzly bears and humans is like no other human-animal dynamic in nature. Grizzly bears look at humans differently from any other large mammalian species. Extremely intuitive, they view some animals—particularly predators such as wolves and other bears—as competition or threats. They view most ungulates and smaller animals as potential food. However with human beings, it's a different story. Grizzlies generally have a cautious respect and a healthy fear of us humans whether innate, or learned from experiences or parental training.

On the other hand, many bears in protected areas have realized that humans may not be a threat but a tolerable nuisance. Some become comfortable spending time in close proximity to unarmed people. These bruins usually look at people as neutral, neither threat nor friend, as they go about their business of packing on fat for the long winter. Being near humans also gives them some protection from the danger of larger, more dominant bears whose shyness usually keeps them far from human presence. Some grizzlies, like the mother bear I wrote about earlier, use humans as a shield against the threat from bigger bears. In Yellowstone for example, roadside bears are usually comprised of subordinate family groups or individuals. These particular bears are simply using the roadside corridor as a safety net so they can take advantage of food sources untapped by the vast majority of the bear population, who remain deeply wary of getting too close to human activity.

The bottom line is that bears are individuals: there are intelligent ones and a few stupid ones. However, I believe that most view us as superior beings, and their reactions toward us are generally very different from their reactions toward the animals that live in their world. To grizzlies, humans usually mean trouble, and the best we should hope for is a watchful truce that allows us to view these incredible creatures in their natural world while keeping them at a safe distance that ensures their safety and their wise apprehension about human beings and our actions.

I believe we need the grizzly bear, and I'm not just talking about people like myself whose lives are built around the study of the marvelous animals. I'm talking about all of us. I think we need the grizzly in the same way that we need places like the Arctic National Wildlife Refuge (ANWR), which has been the subject of so much controversy over potential oil drilling. Places like ANWR and creatures like the grizzly are vital to human health and happiness, even if many of us never set foot in Alaska or see a bear anyplace but on television. Just knowing that such wild majesty and untouched natural beauty still exists in this world is like a tonic for the soul. That knowledge has a far-reaching effect on the human psyche. It's as if we know that as long as such creatures walk the earth and places remain unspoiled, there's hope for us and our future.

This is why I'm a teacher, first and foremost. My greatest hope (and the grizzly's) lies in education transforming public perception, helping people to understand the true nature of the grizzly bear and its fragile and irreplaceable role in the North American wilderness. I hope to inspire more people to think like the great Chief Seattle, who said in 1853:

This we know. The Earth does not belong to man; man belongs to the Earth. This we know. All things are connected like blood, which unites one family. All things are connected. Whatever befalls the Earth befalls the sons of the Earth. Man did not weave the web of life; he is merely a strand in it. Whatever he does to the web, he does to himself.

3

From White Sox Country to Grizzly Country

She flew like a champ on her flight to freedom
The Empress would not be denied
I knew she would make it the first time I saw her
I could tell by the look in her eye
Yes, I knew she would make it the first time I saw her
I could tell by the look in her eye

—"The Empress," music and lyrics by James R. Cole

McNEIL RIVER STATE GAME SANCTUARY, ALASKA—JULY 1990

A DOZEN PHOTOGRAPHERS RIVETED their lenses upon the bears jockeying for prime fishing spots through the cascading waterfalls below. We were huddled together on a dirt viewing pad with no physical barriers between human observers and more than fifty brown bears. As I stood on the far right edge of the group, I felt a slight nudge on my right hip and turned my head away from the camera: a sub-adult grizzly had edged past me. His head was up and alert, his eyes carefully checking out the river. He wasn't concerned about our presence at all; this bruin was focused solely on coming away with a juicy chum salmon while avoiding the potential danger posed by the more dominant bears, particularly the big males. The safety record in this sanctuary is unblemished, as these bears have learned to trust humans and view us as benign, neutral objects. While the young bear continued warily down the hillside, I continued my viewing and photography. He never even looked back my way.

That was just one of hundreds of encounters I've been blessed to have over the years. How I ended up in Montana, devoting my life to studying grizzly bears and eventually coming face to fur with my second attacking bear is the story of my lifetime.

From the time I was four-and-a-half years old until I was eighteen, I lived in Highland Park, Illinois, outside Chicago. It was a typical 1950s suburban environment, with Italians and Jews segregated into their own neighborhoods but mingling freely. We were mostly spared the still-lingering anti-Semitism of the time because my father had changed his name from Cohen to Cole after getting out of the Navy in 1946. I can only assume he did it to give himself and his future family the chance to succeed or fail based on their own hard work, and as with just about everything else in my life, I'm grateful to him for it.

I was always an active, athletic, independent, and sometimes stubborn kid. Only one time did this come close to getting me in serious trouble. On some weekdays, I would skip school and go to downtown Chicago with my father to go to banks and look for rare coins. On those trips, I would often journey on foot across "The Loop" to visit my Uncle Mort, who sold Contour Chairs. Along the way, I would run like a Chicago Bears running back along the sidewalk, faking my way between pedestrians, who were oblivious to the fact that I was about to break the single-season rushing record, except when traffic lights forced me to stop.

One time, when I must have been eleven or twelve years old, I out-faked myself and ran smack into a seemingly innocent bystander. We both went to the sidewalk like a ton of bricks. As I lay there two big men helped the victim to his feet and passersby, one by one, tipped their hat and said, "Good morning Mr. Mayor." I gasped. I had just sacked Mayor Richard J. Daley, head of the infamous Chicago political machine and probably the most powerful Democrat in the country other than the president. Fortunately, I was still an innocent-looking child, so nobody said a word to me as the mayor put his hat back on and walked off with his bodyguards. After that, I was a lot more careful on my sidewalk rushing plays.

I come from a long line of road trippers. Don't get me wrong: I live for hiking through the backcountry. I have an active, sometimes hyperactive mind that worries and analyzes and keeps me awake even when my body is exhausted after a twenty-five-mile hike, but out in grizzly bear country, I feel at peace. When I get out there with a pack on my back, even if I don't see a bear (which happens often), I feel at home and sleep like a log. But I also adore driving and being on the road; it's a tonic to my restless mind. I have no doubt that my affection for the open road comes from the many road trips through the West that my dad would take my sister, Tootsie, and me on when we were kids.

In the late 1930s, my father, my Uncle Mort, and my grandfather Michael Cohen embarked on an epic round-trip journey from Chicago to California. Dad said this exploration of the West took several weeks, including a handful of stops to visit family along the way, and lit a fire in my father that burned brightly right up to the very last day of his life. He always loved to drive, loved the open road, and loved to head out West, as do I.

Long before I reached legal driving age, Dad took my sister and me along with Peppy, our miniature Schnauzer who faithfully slept on his lap, on long winter road trips to Denver and Phoenix to visit relatives during the Christmas holidays. My father and I were avid numismatists—collectors of rare coins—so these trips also became coin prospecting junkets. Talk about a great time for a young boy! I already told you about playing hooky to head downtown with Dad. Well, when we got off the train, Dad went to his office while I went to the biggest banks in Chicago and spent my days picking through rolls of coins at Continental Bank, Harris Bank, and The Northern Trust. By age twelve, I was on a first name basis with the tellers—and I had identified many a rare coin that became part of our collection. This local coin collecting soon became our favorite on-the-road diversion.

On our western winter road trips, we brought along dozens

of rolls of pennies, nickels, dimes, quarters, and half dollars. This roving numismatic office stopped at banks along our route to exchange our rolls for theirs. Then, as Dad tooled down the interstate, my sister and I sat in the back seat with a big tray between us and sorted through all the new rolls to search out coins whose age or rarity gave them a worth beyond their face value. I was a knowledgeable numismatist at the time and could quickly recognize any worthwhile coin. Each time we took a coin out of a bank roll, I replaced it with a coin of the same denomination from our "filler" pile so we would always have rolls with the right coin count to exchange at the next bank. Any time Tootsie or I found a valuable coin, we passed the news up to the front seat and the three of us shared a satisfying moment. Then it was on to the next town and the next bank. This family tradition continued for so many years that we got to know various local bank presidents and tellers in the towns along our driving routes. It was a wonderful way to learn and pass the time on the West's long highways. It ended up being lucrative, too: we eventually sold the collection and my share was enough to put a substantial down payment on a house I bought in Boulder, Colorado, in 1978.

In the meantime, I was falling in love with the West. The best part of these annual cross-country adventures was exploring everything along the way. With Dad's steady hand at the wheel, we braved all kinds of winter weather—from ice storms in Nebraska to heavy snow through the northern New Mexico mountains near Taos. People have asked me how I managed to stay so calm and cool after both my bear maulings, and at least part of my answer is, I learned it from my dad! We drove through some scary conditions on those trips, including creeping along roads where the fog was so thick that my father had to drive with his head out the window to follow the yellow line. Not once did he ever show a moment of panic or even concern. He was as cool as the proverbial cucumber.

There were certainly some tenuous circumstances to contend with during our winter travels, but they were part of the journey; we thrived on the adventure. But as the years went along and I became more enamored of the West, I started to crave my own brand of exploration, driving or hiking and finding my own way, seeing things from my own perspective. That impulse and my early Wisconsin wildlife experiences were beginning to blend into an irresistible call toward the Mountain West.

In some ways, this book is not just a chronicle of my grizzly attacks and a call for greater education and preservation of their natural habitat. It's also a love letter to my dad, who was and remains the most important person in my life, even though he's gone. But I also had a mom who gave me everything a boy could ask for, though she never had a terribly happy life herself.

My mother's life was fraught with addictions: cigarettes, prescription medication, and alcohol, though she didn't take a drink in the last fifteen years of her life. Continuous health problems, one on top of the other, plagued her. A complete lack of physical exercise was a heavy contributor to a severe case of osteoporosis that she developed in her later years. She was a champ at taking care of others, but not so good at taking care of herself.

When I was fourteen, my parents separated, which I think is always shocking to a child. Two years later they would divorce. Something like this was supposed to happen to other families, not mine. They must have been conducting their personal matters behind closed doors because I never saw them fight; they rarely even argued in front of us. I just never saw it coming. Mom's health was deteriorating by this time, and her second marriage didn't help matters. She had a wonderful, zany sense of humor, but there wasn't much to laugh about anymore.

Fortunately for us, my parents maintained a solid friendship after their divorce. They were forced to hide this from their new spouses, but they never hesitated to communicate on any matter that concerned their children. I always had total trust in both my parents. When I needed advice, who better to ask? They were usually in agreement on most issues and I usually followed their advice.

The highlight of my mother's year was a visit to my home in Colorado, where I lived as an adult. After one trip when my sister and I were still living together, she sent the following letter:

My Darling Daughter and Son:

Yep, this is one of my "hearts and flowers" letters, but one I feel I must write!

The weekend we spent together was the most wonderful

period of time I can ever remember. I was literally bursting with pride talking with you and hearing all your thoughts, ideas, and seeing your ability to cope with problems at your young ages. It was most amazing to me because you both have now what most people strive for all their lives and never attain. You really have it together!

I want to thank you for sharing your life and dreams with me and for making me so welcome in your home! I do not have to tell you what it meant to me!

I could ramble on and on about my two great children, but to sum it up—I am very proud and very happy to be fortunate enough to be able to say I am your Mother!

All my love always, Mom

The last time I saw my mother healthy was on my fortieth birthday. We secretly met Dad at a nice restaurant in downtown Chicago. Mom asked me ahead of time if I would promise not to get emotional, but it was too much. Dad held the chair for Mom and it was so comfortable, like old times. January 4, 1990, was by far the greatest birthday of my life, though I never even told my sister about it until many years had passed.

Later that year, my mother's difficult life ended with heart failure at sixty-three. She passed on before my Montana years and never saw a grizzly, although we often toured through Rocky Mountain National Park when she came to Boulder. She was a tough, loving mother who passed both qualities, thankfully, on to me.

My father was really the fulcrum of my life, though. The

strong legs that have propelled me over tens of thousands of miles of trails in Montana, Wyoming, Colorado, Alaska, and more of the most breathtakingly rugged country of the West are his legacy. Even overweight and in old age, his legs were powerful. Some of my most memorable times were spent with him. Later in his life, when he was in semi-retirement, he bought a second home in Rancho Mirage, California, near Palm Springs. There he could relax, enjoy the warm weather, and still conduct business by phone when he needed to. Most important, he could play golf year-round. Besides instilling a passion for baseball in me (I am still a huge White Sox fan), Dad was also a terrific athlete. He was offered a minor league contract with the White Sox once upon a time and was captain of his high school basketball team, though he couldn't go to college because his family couldn't afford it. But as far as golf was concerned, he was a lifer. In fact, he nailed his fifth hole in one during the last week of his life.

Dad lived out his dreams the same way I live mine; they were just a whole different set of dreams. For him, the dream of dreams was to own a Cadillac. He owned many through the years, and he would take care of each one like it was a prized jewel. He rarely took them to a car wash, but instead washed them by hand. He almost always had a convertible, and when the new models came out—back when there was a set time when the next year's new cars were rolled out—it was always hard for him to part with the old one. But every four or five years, he did.

Back in the eighties, the California (now Los Angeles)

Angels were training in Palm Springs, not far from where my father had bought his house. I would time my visits so we could go to a spring training game or practice. One of my most vivid memories was going to a morning practice, followed by a lunch break, and then an intra-squad game in the afternoon. This is baseball for the true devotee: practicing fundamentals, nothing on the line, just the pure beauty of the game. We were driving there in Dad's Caddy convertible with the top down, my father in an old pair of sweat pants. Dad says suddenly, "This is my dream, to be in Southern California in the wintertime, going to spring training with my son, under the blue skies. How could this be better?" We both got emotional. We stayed all morning watching all the drills major leaguers do. We ate lunch on the lawn and played catch with a sixteen-inch softball. It was an incredible trip.

Even before I entered high school, I knew that my life would not be spent in Illinois. I loved mountains and the "Land of Lincoln" lacked mountains and bears. In those days, I was what today would be called a "multi-sport athlete." Though my favorite sport was baseball, I played number-one singles on my high school tennis team, and I shined in part because tennis had not yet become popular so the overall competition was relatively weak. I got by on sheer athleticism; I never took lessons and my game was by no means polished, powerful, or dominant, but I was a fierce competitor like my father. Meanwhile, my tennis teaching career began with a low-budget advertisement in the local newspaper. By eighteen, I was head tennis professional at a lavish country club, a position I held for three summers and which would follow me on my travels west, providing both income and opportunity.

When it came time to choose a college, my eyes only turned toward the sunset. I wanted rugged country where I could enjoy natural beauty and great hiking, so with my sights set on the Rocky Mountains, I applied to the University of Colorado (CU) in Boulder. My grades had not been stellar, mostly because my mercurial mind didn't really take to "book learning"; I would rather be out in the world, getting my hands dirty and learning by doing. I have nothing but respect for university education, but that's just the way I'm wired. Anyway, I was accepted on the condition that I successfully complete a five-week summer school class as a prerequisite for full time enrollment in the fall. So my college career began at the foot of the Rocky Mountains as I became acquainted with this charming college town. Summer school was hard work, a lot of fun, and convinced me that this was the right place to be. But it didn't take long for me to figure out that complete freedom in Colorado meant having a car.

So back in Chicago for the summer of '68, I worked three jobs to meet my goal of buying a car free and clear and paying for a year's insurance. My father could easily have afforded to buy me a car, but he chose not to. The idea was for me to learn to make my own way in the world. He was already giving me the opportunity for a college education by paying my hefty out-of-state tuition plus room and board. If I wanted a car, I would have to earn it. Dad's reasoning was that this sense of accomplishment would help build my confidence and self-esteem, and as usual, he was right. Just a few days after the fateful 1968 Democratic convention, I headed back to Boulder on Interstate 80 in a used red Oldsmobile Cutlass with a black vinyl top, which would be my wheels for the next five years.

Car goal reached, I settled into a routine of classes, tennis, and music at the University of Colorado. My initial major was business for no reason other than that my dad was in business, real estate to be specific. As I said, I was never very motivated in the classroom. But music became a passion, thanks to my friend Al Johnson, who has been known since then as "Suitcase Simpson" (or simply "Simps"), because of his enormous white suitcase that inspired me to name him after an often-traded baseball journeyman. Simps was also my tennis doubles partner and roommate, and was a good singer who accompanied himself with the rhythm guitar. We had a ball singing together for friends and at parties.

Now, my father was one of the most musical persons I have ever known. He would play music in the house all the time when I was growing up: Sinatra, Jolson, Sammy Davis Jr., to name a few. Any time he whistled or hummed to a song, he was in perfect tune. When I would play my original songs for him, he would critique them. He talked about taking up the tenor banjo and never did, but he had superb musical taste and an impeccable ear.

He obviously infected me with his love of music, because it wasn't long before I was bugging Simps almost every night to abandon his studies (he majored in physics) so that we could rehearse songs. It wasn't hard to pull him away from the books, but I'm sure his grades suffered. After a while, I felt guilty and asked him to teach me how to play the guitar. Graciously, he showed me all of the basic chord progressions, and my fanatical practicing quickly dominated all of my spare moments. By Thanksgiving vacation of 1970, when my new musical skills were only about a month old, I was able to respectably perform a handful of songs for family and friends back in Highland Park. It probably didn't sound too good, but for me, this was quite an accomplishment. Singing, writing songs, and playing guitar, banjo, and mandolin have become integral parts of my everyday life.

As I said, I've always been an independent thinker and lived in the way that feels right to me, no matter what anyone else may think about it. In part because of that independent streak, life in Colorado was perfect for me as the 1970s rolled in. I was playing intercollegiate tennis and teaming in doubles with my good friend Bill Edelman. We would travel to the West Coast in the early spring to play the best teams in the country, which was a perfect tune-up for the teams of the Big Eight, the conference CU was in. In fact, during my tennis career I actually became the center of controversy because I wore my hair long and in a ponytail. If you can believe it, this was a big deal in the conservative world of college tennis. I was almost banned from tournaments because of my hair; I am nearly certain that I was the first (male) collegiate player in any major sport in the country to play with a ponytail.

Teaching tennis was my livelihood through the 1970s, mostly in Boulder, but highlighted by three marvelous winters in the southern Arizona desert working alongside Australian legends Margaret Court and Fred Stolle at the Tucson Racket Club Ranch. Ms. Court was very modest and was not very demonstrative, but incredibly astute about tennis. Stolle was her exact opposite, the stereotypical Aussie: really outgoing, humorous, and demonstrative. He had a house in the Tucson foothills and would hang out with us. I wanted to learn some Aussie songs and so he told me to come to his house, and I learned "Waltzing Matilda," among others. What a great guy.

After five years of enjoying the tamed mountain splendor of Boulder, my inner mountain man revealed himself on my first trip to Glacier National Park in September 1973. The place absolutely took my breath away and left me speechless—no mean feat for a chatterbox like me. The dramatic peaks, lush valleys, and abundant wildlife on the "Crown of the Continent" called to me like nothing else had. Hiking the same soil with grizzly bears gave every step a *frisson* of excitement. Later in the trip, a lone black bear visited my car campground at Bowman Lake in the northwest corner of the park; it was my first wild bruin sighting since Camp Menominee. In my wildest dreams I had never envisioned a place so spectacular with such beauty. I was hooked, hopelessly and forever.

The following year, my stepbrother Beau turned me on to the book *Grizzly Country* by Andy Russell, father of the great bear expert Charlie Russell. To this day, this book stands tall as one of the best ever written about grizzly bears. It taught me so much about these fascinating creatures that was beyond the myth and fear commonly fostered by the public. Then, in November 1975, when my sister, Tootsie, and I cruised the east side of Going-to-the-Sun Road in Glacier Park in my orange 1963 Chevy truck, I had the first grizzly sighting that I've already told you about.

With that, my annual trips to Glacier and Yellowstone became bi-annual then tri-annual. The more I hiked through Glacier, the more I learned about grizzly habitat and sign. I spotted some grizzlies, but they were few and far between, especially in the early years. I spent some Christmas vacations in a cabin with a woodstove or at a hostel near the Canadian border just outside of the park. Cross country skiing became a classroom for learning about animal tracking, learning to spot the signs of coyotes, mountain lions, lynx, wolves, and other predators passing. My mind was opening to an incredible world that I knew I had to be a part of.

From that time on, wilderness and wild creatures became the centers of my world. My first trip to Alaska came in 1979, courtesy of the Alaska Marine Highway System, a three-day cruise from Seattle to Juneau for $95 one-way. One-way was all I cared about for a while; I was in the enviable position of being a single man without any responsibilities and I wanted to see some wonders. I wasn't disappointed. I flew from Juneau to Anchorage, was dropped off in the highlands, and it took six hours and two rides to hitchhike the 240 miles to what was then called Mount McKinley National Park. I was there in cool September weather, and cars didn't come along more often than every half hour or so. As rain was pelting down, I was under my poncho playing my harmonica and trying to flag down another ride. It was a dreary, frustrating day until finally, a jolly fellow named Jerry Nebel stopped and said, "What are you up to?" I told him I was going into the park; so was he. I jumped in and a friendship was formed.

Our karma was incredible. We were friends in minutes, and we are to this day. Well, we got an hour into the park and I looked up on the hillside above the road and saw a beautiful blond grizzly bear foraging. I didn't own a camera at that point; taking photos wasn't even on my mind. I'm a self-taught photographer who didn't get my first camera until my mother bought me a Canon AE-1 for Christmas in 1979. I bought a zoom lens and set out to learn on my own. That's how I'm happiest: try something, mess up, figure out what I did wrong, learn, repeat. In 2007 I finally broke down and bought myself a Canon digital camera, which has been a revelation. If I knew more about all the gadgets on that camera, I suppose I would be a better photographer, but I'm happy with the work I've done.

Anyway, I had never seen a bear like that one, out in the open for so long. It was harder to find them in Glacier and Yellowstone. The grizzly didn't seem disturbed, even with people stopping to watch. We stayed there for two or three hours, and I knew I had to see more. After a couple of days of camping, Jerry dropped me off and I connected with a couple of girls whom I had met on the boat north. They had told me they had a friend who was a park ranger, and said if I played my cards right, the ranger and his wife might let me stay with them in the heart of the park. I was on a wing and a prayer— what did I have to lose?

The ranger, his wife, and the girls picked me up and we went into the park for the day, then to their cabin. It turned out that my connection with the park ranger and his wife was very strong—as strong as with Jerry. I picked up their guitar and played some tunes and they asked me to stay for dinner. Then after dinner they asked me to stay the night. By the time the evening was over, they asked me to stay indefinitely.

So the girls left and I stayed for a couple of weeks. The ranger even loaned me his Jeep to drive through the park and gave me tips on where to see bears. This was one of the greatest periods of my life. I became part of this little ranger community. I got to know other rangers' kids, took the sled dogs out for walks, and went to other people's cabins for social events. I learned an immense amount. The community was remote: 120 miles from Fairbanks, where the nearest grocery stores were. They would all go to town about once a month and buy huge amounts of groceries, and the running joke was that their friends would put on weight whenever they came to stay. But I didn't. Without a trail system, I was bushwhacking miles every day across the rolling, spongy tundra. I was in heaven.

By 1980, a fire was burning inside me. I knew that I wanted to spend my life working with and learning about wild creatures—especially the majestic grizzly bear—and living in what remained of the untouched North American wilderness. But there was one small obstacle: money. I wasn't ever going to make enough of it teaching tennis. So by 1982 I had abandoned professional tennis and embarked on a career as a commercial real estate agent in Boulder.

I wasn't unfamiliar with real estate. My father had operated a successful one-man real estate firm, "Robert C. Cole and Company," since 1953. He remained in the real estate business for fifty-one years up until the day he died. To him this was "the greatest business in the world," offering independence and a flexible schedule as well as potentially unlimited earning power. Dad wanted me to join him in the business but ultimately I said "no" to Chicago. I wanted to be in the West, closer to my ultimate vision: my move to Montana. Real estate wasn't really for me, but I was naturally good at it and it could be the means to an end. It could give me the freedom to do what I wanted. I planned to make money and sock it away and buy myself freedom at a young age.

(I was already preparing for my life-changing move. When an episode of *The Honeymooners*, a Marx Brothers movie, a favorite old film, or a wildlife program came on, I would videotape it. When my friends teased me about my growing library of tapes, I told them that I was preparing for the day when I lived in a cabin in Montana without any television reception. I don't think anyone believed me.)

Richard Berman, my great friend and surrogate brother who plays a pivotal role later in this story, finally convinced me to become a commercial leasing agent in his new company, The Colorado Group. In the beginning when I studied for my real estate license exam, Richard and I shared a small office. I've never shared an office with anybody in such close quarters before or since, but we got along great, a sign of things to come.

The anchor of my early business success was cold calls. Never one to be shy, I systematically knocked on the door of every business I could find in Boulder. Multiple deals and business contacts came from this, including the two biggest deals of my real estate career. The first year I made more money than I had ever made in my life. After the second year, I had one foot out the door—facing Montana and my ideal life.

My workdays usually started with a glorious mountain run in the early morning (I was and am absolutely fanatical about fitness and taking care of my body), followed by a shower, breakfast, and a five-minute drive to the office. Life was rich and varied. I had four groups of friends who rarely crossed paths unless I threw a big party: music friends, outdoor activity friends, tennis friends, and real estate friends. On weekends, I'd be up at 3 A.M. so I could be at Rocky Mountain National Park at dawn and have the trails to myself for fifteen miles. It meant I could see more wildlife. I was so busy during these years that I only ventured to Alaska in 1985 and 1990, even though I went to Glacier and Yellowstone as often as I could.

But all of this just wasn't enough. My friends and family thought I had it made. Here I was living in this magical town at the edge of the Rocky Mountains and making a fine living. But I took little satisfaction when I closed big real estate deals except for collecting my commission and depositing it in the bank. My superficially successful lifestyle looked great on paper, but didn't come close to fulfilling my innermost needs. I knew I was working on my dramatic life change, but I also knew it would be hard to keep my passion for Montana and the grizzlies in check while I saved and planned.

Besides my great friends, the best parts of my life in Boulder were my work with wildlife. During my final three years in real estate, I held down two part-time volunteer jobs. One of them entailed working with my friend Michael Sanders for Boulder County Parks and Open Space assisting him with public education and documentation of mountain lion and black bear activity in the front-range area. Though I never saw a single mountain lion or black bear in the Boulder area, I interviewed many people who shared riveting stories about their encounters.

My other animal-related job gave me the privilege of working with the great Sigrid Ueblacker and her Birds of Prey Rehabilitation Foundation. The work was often bittersweet but in the end, it was incredibly rewarding. I learned that humans left their mark on almost every raptor injury. Being shot, ingesting poison, or flying into plate glass windows or power lines were common reasons the birds landed in our care. On too many occasions, I held an incurably wounded bird in my arms while

Sigrid administered the euthanasia shot. However, we successfully released into the wild two out of every three birds that
came into the facility. I cared for injured raptors of all breeds, but
one spectacular golden eagle made a special lasting impression.

Downtrodden and apparently near death from severe poi-
soning, the bird called "The Empress" entered our facility. She
was like no other bird I have ever seen. She would look at me
in a way that I have never had a bird look at me. She had a
spunk to her, and no one else could get near her. I would
slowly walk over to her and put my hands on top of her talons
and stroke her feathers, which was seemingly dangerous when
she was not restricted in any way. I would never have thought
about doing this with another bird, but her body language
was completely calm and unthreatening toward me. She could
have severely injured my hand with her powerful talons, but
she never harmed me. As she became stronger and graduated
into the big flight cage, she regained her independence and
wouldn't let anyone come close to her, including me. That
was as it should have been. She was later successfully released
back into the wilderness.

Sigrid passed away in late 2009, but her legacy lives on. She
had a special gift and was totally dedicated to what she did.
She treated each injured raptor like her child. I feel truly lucky
to have worked so closely with her. We need more Sigrids in
the world.

I had gotten into real estate in 1982. In October 1985, I was
still in the business, still saving. Had I become a little bit
complacent about my dream? I don't know, but something

happened that woke me up in a harsh way: my close friend Merle Watson died suddenly in a tractor accident in a North Carolina forest at age thirty-six.

I had met Merle and his father, the blind folk and roots guitar legend Arthel "Doc" Watson, back in December 1972. In the autumn of that year, I laid my ears on a live double album on the old Vanguard label, *Doc and Merle Watson—On Stage*. Right out of the chute I was magnetically drawn to the folksy acoustic music style of this incredible duo. They were scheduled to perform concerts on four consecutive nights the following December at Tulagi's nightclub near the University of Colorado campus. I bought tickets for all four shows.

On opening night, I was among the first in line. I knew that the policy there allowed open seating, so I chose a prime spot, front row center. Then a girl walked up and said, "They're back there rehearsing in the dressing room with the door open!" I sprung out of my seat to check it out. The crowd was six deep at the dressing room door and although I could hear the music, I couldn't see a thing. I elbowed my way to the front, took one look at Merle sitting on the well-worn dressing room couch playing his Gallagher guitar, then walked right in and sat on the couch next to him. I'm not shy, but I don't know what came over me at that moment.

When the rehearsal song concluded, Merle and I introduced ourselves to each other and I also met Doc for the first time. Merle and I started talking and it was like we had been friends for years. He offered up his guitar and I tried it out. I attended all four concerts and was backstage before and after every show. The following year they played four nights at Ebbets Field, a new Denver nightclub that was founded by the former owner of Tulagi's, and Merle gave my sister, Tootsie, and me free tickets and unlimited backstage access.

Eddy Merle Watson grew up in Deep Gap in the scenic Blue Ridge Mountains of North Carolina, and was named after two of his father's all-time favorite musicians, Eddy Arnold and Merle Travis. At fifteen, after guitar lessons from his mother, Merle joined his father playing music on the road. He was a natural, learning to play the music much quicker than his father did. In the early days, he primarily played backup. But as the years went by, he became a masterful musician in his own right and the perfect complement to his charismatic, hammy father.

Merle would tell me stories about staying up all night playing guitar with the legendary Mississippi John Hurt. He was also inspired to learn slide guitar after listening to Duane Allman of the Allman Brothers Band. Merle became the cleanest and finest slide guitar player I have ever heard—playing slide with a Sears socket wrench. It's true. One day in Milwaukee, Wisconsin, I was with him when he marched right into the Sears tool department, purchased the 5/8-inch Craftsman socket wrench for his ring finger, then used it to play red hot licks on all of the slide tunes during the concert that night.

Merle was a quiet soul who never cared for the limelight. His warm, gentle personality was reserved mostly for family and friends. He was generous to a fault and had impeccable comedic timing. He could fix anything—including my orange

1963 Chevy panel truck, which he did during long, memorable road trips. We shared many great times over the years.

Then just over three years after Merle died, my lifetime tennis partner and close friend Bill Edelman died of cancer in February 1989. He was also thirty-six. This was just too much to handle. I was badly shaken. Bill had two funerals—one in Colorado, a memorial the day after he died—and then his parents took his body back to New Jersey. He had liver cancer and we had known for a while that he wasn't going to make it, but the finality of his passing was difficult. I was in my office when I got the call on February 1, 1989 that Bill had passed. I quickly told my colleagues that I wasn't going to be around for a couple of days, drove down to meet his parents at his townhouse in south Denver, spent time with them and then slept in Bill's bed that night. The next day was the memorial. Bill had requested that people who had something to say should get up and say it. A lot of people got up and shared their memories, but I wasn't one of them; there was no way I could have uttered a word.

After Bill's death, the oft-mentioned phrase that "life can be short" hit me square in the face. What was I waiting for? I was studying grizzlies part-time with frequent trips to Montana, Wyoming, and Alaska, but it just wasn't enough. Why couldn't I follow my passion and live out my dreams now, while I was still young and physically able? By this time, my business had gotten a lot easier. Clients were knocking on my door instead of the other way around. Nonetheless, I wasn't happy and would never have been, even if I had earned a million dollars. From the day that Bill died, I had one-and-a-half feet out the door; my goal was to be completely out of real estate by age forty. My game plan was to spend as little as I could, save everything I could, then purchase myself the most precious commodity there is: time. Time to do what I had longed to do for so long. Time to be with family and friends. Time to follow my passions and dreams. Time to follow the great bear through his wilderness home full-time. Time to live.

I had always been a frugal person, so I really didn't have to change much about my spending habits. Some people might want to work their lives away doing what they hate to have a second home or jewelry, but that's never been right for me. What had changed for me was the sense of urgency. My last obstacle was closing my final giant real estate deal.

I needed this deal to close before I could comfortably take my other foot completely out of the door, although I would have seen my business commitment through to the end no matter what. It was a new headquarters for Hauser Chemical Research (HCR), a company that produced, among other things, new anti-cancer agents for drug companies.

Working in an unusual team arrangement with an agent with whom I had formerly been competing for this client, I pieced together the details for a huge custom design and construction deal in a process that took over two years from start to finish. The HCR folks were some of the finest people I've ever worked with in real estate.

The deal finally closed in 1990, paving the way for the beautiful new HCR facility to open its doors a few years later. It was testament to all of the good people who made it happen, and a win-win all the way around. Everybody was happy. My last real estate commission was a whopper. I tendered my letter of resignation effective December 1, 1990. I was unemployed and couldn't have been happier. One client cried when I broke the news, but I was singing. I had accomplished my goal within a month of my forty-first birthday.

Three days later, my mother passed away. The joy of freedom quickly turned to sorrow and despair. I cancelled my next Glacier trip. I went back to Chicago for two-and-a-half weeks to attend her funeral and be with my sister, and then I came back to Boulder and spent the holidays there in deep grief. I knew that death had ended my mother's suffering, but I couldn't help but feel that her life had ended too soon. My head was all over the place for months. I went up to Glacier to work on a wolf research project there. I wandered back to Boulder and stayed for a month or two. I was in a funk.

But by summer, the pilot light on my internal fire re-lit. I headed out for Montana and I was like a kid let loose in Disneyland. I wanted to hike every trail. I would get trail books and plan hikes and backpacking trips. I wanted to see these places, and see them without worrying about calling into the office. On past trips to Glacier and Yellowstone, I always called the office even if I couldn't do anything. The only time I let go of the office was when I went to Alaska because in the deep Alaskan bush, there were no phones. But no more. I lived in a little cabin that cost $275 a month, right on the edge of the park, with wildlife all around me, met the people who lived in the area, and had unlimited access to Glacier Park. I was receiving substantial rental income from my Boulder house, so I was actually making money while doing what I loved. I thought I'd died and really gone to heaven this time.

After my move to Montana I never looked back, not once. Most of that initial winter of freedom after mom died was spent documenting the natural recovery of wolves along the west side of Glacier National Park. I learned from numerous wilderness sojourns with wolf lady Diane Boyd and my late, great friend and musician partner Mike Fairchild, who died suddenly at forty-three in 1996. Michael gave me field tracking lessons through the virgin North Fork snow almost every day; we ate elk from the freezer and picked guitar and mandolin tunes at night by the woodstove. On one day off I skied six miles up to Bowman Lake and deposited my mother's ashes on this magnificent, frozen body of water so that she could rest in peace in the land that I loved.

That summer of 1991 was a dream come true. I lived in a cabin at the confluence of the Middle Fork and the North Fork of the mighty Flathead River, just outside the boundary of Glacier National Park. Every day was Christmas. I took full advantage to really breathe in and explore this wondrous ecosystem. Less than a year after my departure from Boulder, I received the following letter from a business acquaintance:

Dear Jim,

I'm writing mostly because I'm curious about how it feels to have left the rat race. I have strong feelings myself about backing out of city life and beating a hasty retreat to work that's closer to the earth, but it has occurred to me that maybe it's just a fantasy that one can escape to any saner place. I'm very interested to know what your experience has been like.

Are you happier? Do you like the people you work with better, or are there just as many assholes in the park service (or whatever agency you're connected with)? Is there more peace in what you're doing, or are the pressures still there, only different? Do you miss much about living in Boulder, or are you happy in a less populated place? Are you glad you made the change, or was it a mistake? Do you see a future in what you're doing? What's the best thing about having left Boulder and your job here? What's the hardest adjustment you've had to make?

All of these questions were easy to answer. I loved what I was doing, and missed nothing about Boulder except family and friends. In a way, the letter was sadly poignant; clearly, the writer had a deep desire to do what I had done. But most people don't do what I've done for various reasons, all of them valid: family, health, money, connections, fear. I felt proud that I'd had the courage to follow my passion and leave the rat race for good.

The following winter I got serious backcountry experience working alongside the great mountain lion guru Kerry Murphy on the Yellowstone Lion Project. We tracked, captured, and radio-collared mountain lions in northern Yellowstone to establish population dynamics and home range habitat requirements in addition to DNA studies. I was soaking up knowledge and becoming more and more in harmony with my new environment.

A musician who was having guitar tuning problems once said, "Strings are like people: they change and they change and when they stop changing, they die." I suppose I had been like that—I needed to change my life. For the next sixteen years, marred only temporarily by the 1993 mauling in Glacier, I savored every day in the backcountry. In 1998, I relocated to Bozeman, Montana, and subsequently published two books of my photos and bear accounts. Life was better than good. Time was well spent.

I had moved to Bozeman with my girlfriend and we got our dog, a hound mix named Merle (by far the best dog I ever had and named after Merle Watson) in 2000. We married in 2001, but we just weren't a good match. We began divorce proceedings in 2006, and while the end of my marriage did give me more freedom to roam bear country, it cost me dearly: my ex-wife took my beloved Merle with her after our divorce was finalized in 2008. Not a day goes by that I don't miss him.

The last normal day of my life was May 22, 2007. Late in the afternoon, I had just awoken from another of my daily power naps at a pullout along Mary Bay in Yellowstone. As I popped my head up groggy, I spotted a lone grizzly traveling steadily to the west through the bay as a heavy wet spring snowstorm blanketed his path. He appeared to be the same bear who had chased a bison a couple of weeks before.

In the first week of May, the dark grizzly was foraging near the timber above Steamboat Point on a cool sunny morning. The bruin disappeared into the woods heading west, then emerged back out into the open on the eastern edge of Mary Bay. The young bear was calmly foraging along when he suddenly bolted to the west in pursuit of a lone bison. What a sight it was to witness this chase! It seemed like a game to both animals as their pace remained about equal and the bear never got closer than about fifty yards. At one point the bison waited for the bear to catch up so the game could continue. The bison seemed to be egging him on as the chase stretched almost the entire length of Mary Bay and then onto the park road. I wondered what the bear would do with the much bigger bison if he actually caught up with him. A hungry grizzly is no match for a healthy adult bison.

As I stayed warm and dry in my van as the show continued to pelt down, this soaking wet bruin continued toward the west edge of the bay then disappeared into the darkening landscape.

4

Blindsided

Blinded by the onslaught, but pounding through the sagebrush
I could hardly see my wobbly feet but I was guided by the sun
When I crossed that winding creek that flows under the road
I knew that I would make it, but it's the hardest thing I've ever done.

—"Blindsided," music and lyrics by James R. Cole

IT WAS MAY 23, 2007. Beautiful spring snow was steadily falling as I drove the Grand Loop Road through Yellowstone National Park's Hayden Valley in the early morning. I had just called my old pal Richard Berman at about 7 A.M. to say hello before his first tennis lesson of the day. I told him that it was a glorious snowy morning in Yellowstone, and it really was. I had just completed a thorough glassing all over Hayden Valley from various strategically chosen parking pullouts and the conditions looked fantastic for a day walking in this gorgeous wilderness. The only downer was that I had not spotted a single bear. But I hoped that later I would.

My next order of business was to drive to the Mary Bay/ Fishing Bridge area, on the northern edge of Yellowstone Lake, to look for the mother grizzly and one first-year cub that I had seen in that vicinity two days before. Two more of her cubs had gone missing. My hope was that the mother bear would reunite with one or both of her missing cubs and that park visitors would subsequently have the thrill of observing them happily grazing the early green-up of roots and grasses in picturesque Mary Bay.

I have had many deeply affecting experiences with mother bears and their cubs over the years. For over two weeks in October 1999, I watched a wonderfully animated mother bear raise her three spring cubs. She was extremely cautious, protective, and predictable as they fished the mouth of the river every morning then patrolled the lakeshore before nursing and usually napping on the open beach, where she had a good view of potential danger. They were a joy to watch and they became one of many bear families to which I have developed an emotional attachment.

One morning, these bears were nowhere to be seen. There was still no sign as the day warmed up and I instinctively knew something was wrong. My mind created numerous rationalizations with happy endings to explain why they didn't show up all morning but deep down, I knew the tale would not end happily. I was already dejected when a few hours later, I found the cubs huddled together without their mother. I could not imagine her abandoning them; I eventually pieced the story together. Sometime during the night, a big male grizzly had killed the mother bear, probably while she was trying to protect the cubs. Her body was stashed on an island in the river and even though salmon were plentiful, the male fed on her for several days. Now the cub trio was on its own at a tender age. Their chances for survival were bleak.

Over the next few days, I saw the three cubs several times but they were extremely timid in this dense congregation of bears and weren't getting much food. The dramatic turn of events made me very sad but I documented everything that I saw without interference. Nature can be cruel and I have learned the hard way to take the sweet with the bitter. Those were the rules when I signed on, and they will never change.

I worked my way from Fishing Bridge to Lake Butte Overlook and back again without spotting a single bruin. Although I prefer to spend my time in Yellowstone on foot rather than cruising in a vehicle, the road system here lets me cover so much more ground that it's inevitable to log some car time. Whereas Glacier is a hiker's park, Yellowstone is really designed with drivers in mind. But I wasn't about to drive back and forth all day long; it was a great day in my book and I was aching to get out into open wilderness country.

However, the best hiking around the Yellowstone Lake area was seasonally closed to human-powered travel until July. Bear management personnel wanted to insure that the grizzlies would not be disturbed in their hunting of elk calves in this area during this critical time of the year. I decided to drive back to Hayden Valley to walk the open landscape. My plan was to return later to search for the bear family from the comfort of my van, my home away from home.

Hayden Valley stretches about eight miles west from the park road into the backcountry, bounded by heavy woods and marked with low, undulating hills and ridges. The valley was overcast when I got back, and it had warmed up after the snowy daybreak. The landscape before me was mostly brown. The valley greens up in the spring according to the amount of precipitation, but we were in the ninth year of a regional drought, so any greening would likely be brief. The skies were filled with high clouds and what spring snow had fallen earlier had quickly melted into the landscape, revealing itself to the careful ear as rivulets of trickling water that would eventually find their way into the valley's creek and river system. It would make for slow and marshy going, forcing me to stay higher on the ridgelines to avoid the mud.

The ground was sodden with water and droplets hung down from abundant sagebrush bushes. A hundred years ago, sagebrush was known as "cowboy cologne" because the unwashed ranch hands (who typically only bathed on Saturday evening) would rub sage all over their faces to disguise their stink before they went into town on a Friday night to try their luck with the ladies. I stuck my face into a sagebrush bush and inhaled. The valley smelled like a cowboy cologne counter in the early morning damp.

I typically choose my routes through Hayden Valley at random. I've walked almost every corner of the valley over the years and I know it extremely well, so choosing paths randomly lets me explore terrain from a different perspective and create different routes each time I'm out there. No maintained human trails exist in this section of Yellowstone, except for the Mary Mountain Trail, which runs along the very northern edge of the valley. Today I was intent on a relatively short hike, a six- to ten-mile loop, so that I would have time to drive back to the Yellowstone Lake/Fishing Bridge area and look again for the mother bear and her family. It was going to be a bit routine, my hike through this extremely familiar landscape. But my intimate knowledge of Hayden Valley would become the difference between life and death.

The hilly terrain sloped to the east as I trail blazed into the valley starting at about 8:30 A.M., and the track was muddy as I headed uphill to the west. To the north, the Washburn Range was cloaked in spring snow. I purposefully switched back often on this slippery slope to maintain my footing. On an established trail I wouldn't have had this problem, but if you've ever walked through wet grass, you know how treacherous it can be. It was worth the trouble. The hilltop offered a spectacular view of the valley in all directions. This allowed me to stop from time to time and thoroughly glass all around with the light, powerful binoculars I always carry within easy reach. I didn't spot a single bear. It was looking like a quiet morning in the valley, but that's the way it is sometimes. Every day offers something different. Luck and timing play a significant role in wildlife viewing and I've certainly paid my dues with many bear-less days over the years.

I saw numerous bison, calmly grazing in small groups dotting the valley. The big ungulates are not anywhere near as common in the park as they once were, before fears that they would spread disease to cattle compelled authorities to thin their numbers when they step outside the park boundaries. Not long ago, I would likely have seen larger herds of the 2,000-pound mammals munching the low grasses. In this valley I typically see no more than thirty in a herd and more frequently just a few together. It makes me wonder what the plains and valleys of this region must have been like 200 years ago before the white man virtually exterminated this great animal for its hide. Herds in the hundreds of thousands thundered through the West. It must have been an incredible sight.

Just within the past week, the same grizzly that I saw chasing the bison earlier in the spring took control of a cow elk carcass out in the open in Mary Bay. Witnesses described how wolves took down this elk, barely visible in the early morning light, just beyond the thermal smoke near the west edge of the bay before the bear chased them off. The young bruin was surrounded by ravens for two days and smaller predators constantly challenged his control of the carcass.

Bull bison often approached and the intimidated bear would flee, but he returned when the bison moved on. The bison were obviously not competing for the meat, but they dominated the scene with their sheer size whenever they chose to. Coyotes ambled by and stole scraps when the bear was looking the other way. A wolf lay nearby scoping out the situation. A few times when the bear temporarily left the carcass, the wolf would seize the opportunity to frantically feed, retreating with a meaty elk chunk in its mouth when the bear abruptly returned. When a lone coyote approached, the wolf gave chase. The scavenging canines fed only when the carcass was unguarded, but the grizzly consumed most of the meat and only shared when he had no choice. The carcass drew quite a crowd and was a pleasure to chronicle.

Further to the west I walked through a familiar flat sandy thermal area that reeked of sulfur and billowed with steam coming from holes in the ground. The area was visibly crisscrossed by grizzly bear tracks of various sizes. I stooped to examine the tracks more closely. The only recent prints were mine.

The short grassy areas nearby resembled manicured golf fairways so closely that I have named the area "the golf course" and call the parts with the most perfectly mown turf "the first hole" and "the second hole." Both greens showed evidence of divot-like grizzly diggings from earlier in the spring as the great bears foraged on the lush grasses, edible roots, and tubers. The area is a popular corridor for grizzlies because the thermals melt the snow and green the vegetation earlier than the surrounding hills. But no bear sign that I saw this day was fresh. So far that spring, I had seen at least nine different grizzlies in the valley but there had been no bear sightings that day.

My intended path for my brief hike continued to the west along the northern edge of a swampy meadow, which I carefully avoided to keep my hiking boots dry. Novices to wilderness hiking are often surprised at how much water there is and how wet boots can become, even if you're not forced to walk through a swamp or ford a stream. Even early morning dew can soak your feet. I added miles to my hike in order to avoid the marshy ground and stay on high contour where I could better observe any bears.

My circuitous route took me up and down several ridge-lines that were wonderful for glassing this section of the valley. Plenty of scattered bison, but not a bear in sight. I continued up a small hill toward a stand of fir trees, and my path led me by a small pond, where I saw some waterfowl as I circled around to the south.

Three weeks earlier, along this same route, I had spotted the silhouette of a massive body above the dry landscape. A big male grizzly fed alone on the meager remains of a bison carcass at the edge of a shallow creek. This likely wasn't his first feeding here: dirt partially covered the carrion, a sure sign that he had buried it after a previous feeding to mask the smell from other bears who would be ravenous competition after just emerging from their dens in the early spring.

Big male grizzlies are shy, secretive, and rarely seen by human eyes. Their secluded lifestyle and careful avoidance of people goes a long way toward explaining how they get big and old. The park road would open to motorized vehicles two days later; by that time, this big guy would likely be nowhere to be found. When the wind swirled and he picked up my scent, he turned tail and rambled uphill into the timber to the north. A flock of ravens followed and when he stopped running to look back, they all systematically landed close by. He paid them no mind, as the naked carcass lay far behind.

This day, an apparently easy path lay ahead for me as I made a beeline for a distinct notch between a series of rounded grassy knolls that form a natural partition along the southern part of the valley bisected by Trout Creek. On the other side of these knolls, my glassing ability would be challenged as I tried with my binoculars to spot bears far away in the vast southern reaches of the valley, near the tree line far beyond Trout Creek. To the south, toward the distant, dense woods, a line of thermals sent up steam like a row of campfires. Those woods, I knew, would shelter multiple grizzlies during the day, as the big animals traveled many miles to find safety in the deep forest, often reemerging in the shadows and cool of the evening.

While glassing just three days before in the early morning, I caught a brief glimpse of a big grizzly along this distant tree line just as he began to melt into the forest on the far southern edge of the valley. This could have been the same bear that I saw feeding on the carcass a couple of weeks prior, but he was so far away that I could not tell. The sighting lasted less than a minute before he disappeared.

I headed toward the southern woods, then began to circle back to the east—the general direction where my van was parked. As I was headed up a gentle knoll, I was thinking that it was time to end my bear-less day in Hayden Valley and get back to the van so I could go and look for the mother bear around Mary Bay/Fishing Bridge. There simply didn't seem to be any ursine activity around here, so greener pastures beckoned.

My greatest sin that morning was not making enough noise. My personal hiking strategy in grizzly country is to make plenty of noise in forested areas and dense cover, but generally not much in the open Yellowstone valleys. My preferred form of noise takes full advantage of my ample supply of hot air (or so my friends tell me) and involves random loud vocalizations such as "Yo! Yo!" fired off every fifty to hundred yards or so when I'm in selected topography where visibility is limited. Although I consider myself cautious and conservative when it comes to safety issues, overall I admit to not making enough intentional noise in grizzly country. I have hiked and camped for days, weeks, months out in the wilderness and it's my goal to see wildlife—especially grizzlies—though certainly not via a point blank surprise, which is virtually the only time an experienced backcountry hiker will be in any danger.

To further my "no surprise" strategy, I don't wear camouflage. I want bears to see me so they can evaluate the situation while I do the same. In every instance when I see a grizzly and the bear sees me, I size up the scenario based on how the bear's body language reacts to my presence. Then, based on my experience, I decide where to position myself to maximize observation or photographic opportunities while causing the least disturbance or threat to the bears. As I've said, my goal is to document the animals behaving naturally, not their responses to my blundering presence.

So, with all my years of experience, my attitude might have been a bit complacent on that morning. I may have assumed that because I had not seen any sign of bears so far that there would not be any, which is always a mistake. My best recollection was that I was very alert (as always) but my perpetually overcrowded mind was thinking ahead for a change and mapping out plans for the afternoon. As a result, it's possible that I wasn't as aware of my surroundings as I might have been.

Everyone who shares the turf with the great bear must find his or her own comfort level. My recommendation to grizzly bear enthusiasts is to make noise when appropriate, but not enough to contaminate the experience. I do know that as I crested that fateful knoll, my forward vision was momentarily blocked by a thin, distinct line of sagebrush bushes. As I headed down the south side of the knoll, I was convinced that this would be one more Hayden Valley trek without any bear sightings. It was hard to believe that such a meager open hillock with such low scrub could be concealing anything dangerous.

Though some details are foggy, I have the vivid recollection of descending the gentle sloping knoll and looking first to my left (the southeast), trying to determine the fastest and easiest return route back to my van. In hindsight some people suggested that a carcass may have been close by, but I did not see any scavenging birds like ravens, magpies, or eagles. I am always alert to any carcass sign because a carcass is an obvious draw for a foraging bear.

When I finally glanced back to my right, an angered mother grizzly burst seemingly out of nowhere across the hillside from the west, followed closely by at least one tiny cub. She never made a sound. She came at me at full throttle and at pointblank range, like a silent, furry locomotive. My best recollection is that she was no more than ten to fifteen feet away when I saw her. It all happened so unbelievably quickly that as I look back the scene felt absurdly like one of those western movie ambushes in a box canyon, although this occurred right out in a wide-open space devoid of any significant natural barriers to my vision. The only thing I can chalk it up to is that bears are intelligent creatures adept at making themselves hard to see when they do not want to be seen.

I will never remember exactly what transpired in the next few seconds, but I have done the best I can to piece things together. I was blindsided and there was no time to be frightened. She was on me in an instant and there was nothing I could do except go down quickly, grab my bear spray, and cover my head. I did a poor job across the board. I don't know whether she knocked me down or I went down first, but I suspect that it was a combination of the two. Anyway, I hit the ground in a fight for my life.

Time stood still. I don't know how long the attack lasted. I never felt any pain.

Sometimes, unnerving bear encounters end with nothing more than a feeling of relief mixed with awe—often because the human involved stays cool and does what he or she is supposed to do. One example: a few years back, the early morning sunlight glistened off the calm, mirror-like water near the Continental Divide in Glacier National Park. It was midsummer, with the wild flowers in full bloom; deep red Indian paintbrush dotted the lush landscape. But my tranquil early morning walk along the south shore of a remote alpine lake was rudely interrupted by two rapid huffing sounds close by, like a winded athlete vigorously blowing out air. No such luck; the noise could only be the menacing sound of an agitated bear.

I had two cans of bear spray suspended on my fanny pack belt, and as my head swiveled to the right toward the heavy blast of breathing, my right hand instantaneously drew a can out of one of the holsters, like a gunfighter. There's no point in carrying this bear deterrent if it isn't readily accessible. If you're new to bear country, I highly recommend practicing its use at home a few times: drawing your bear spray from its holster, removing the safety clip, and aiming as if to fire a volley.

As my thumb popped off the plastic safety clip, I saw an angry grizzly barreling toward me from less than forty yards away. With my non-lethal defense weapon armed and ready, I mentally drew a line in the sand approximately fifteen feet away from where I was standing. This bruin would get a snoot full of the mace-like mist only if she crossed that arbitrary boundary into my "Red Zone."

As luck would have it, her charge came to a halt a foot or two shy of the "Red Zone." The agitated mother bear aborted her charge and made an abrupt 180-degree return to her two tiny first-year cubs, who waited anxiously at the edge of the timber about sixty yards away. It had been a bluff charge, a grizzly's emphatic "Get the hell out of here before somebody gets hurt!" gesture. The bear's retreat would normally have been my window of opportunity to back away slowly and try to discretely get out of harm's way while she was preoccupied, so that she would no longer perceive me as a threat to her cubs.

However, I was on the edge of the lakeshore with no place to go, so I stood my ground. The mother bear momentarily checked on her frightened cubs then, apparently not satisfied that this human threat was totally thwarted, turned around again for a second run toward me. This time, she approached right up to the "Red Zone" line. She may have been bluffing again, as she appeared to be turning away, but I couldn't be sure and wasn't taking any chances. *Whoosh!* With one quick shot of red mist toward her face, mom turned tail in a hurry. I don't think she absorbed much of the spray, but sometimes the loud blasting noise of a bear spray canister alone can cause a bear to flee. My knee-jerk assessment was that she was bluffing the second time but I don't know which came first, the spray or the retreat.

The mother grizzly rejoined her nervous cubs, but this time she never broke stride. As she ran past the cubs, they instinctively followed. The dense underbrush quickly swallowed their forms and I never saw them again.

Is it typical for a bear to charge a second time, or a third, or a fourth? Would the mother have completed the second charge

The cowering cub intently watches from a stout branch as its mom faces the potential danger posed by another bear approaching below.

Dexterity and balance are in full display as these siblings spar along the river shore.

Other bears scatter when he enters the river as this dominant 1,200-pound bear has done a superb job filling out his long body frame from when I first saw his as a sub-adult/teenager in 1992.

The bison bull carefully watches the competition between a wolf and a grizzly for a meaty elk carcass in Yellowstone.

A huge bull bison lowers his head as he approaches an elk carcass guarded by a grizzly.

Mom and her small cub make an aquatic retreat while the perceived threat, a mother bear with three two-year-olds, passively watch like slapstick straight men.

A huge male warily crosses rippling rapids in the swift current just below Brooks Falls, Alaska.

A mischievous yearling conducting a canoe inspection looks up at me like a kid with his hand in the cookie jar at the lower Brooks River platform.

An animated spring cub checks out the tourists as he follows mom across the Yellowstone Park road.

This feather is one of many interesting items a curious bear cub will check out during daily travels.

Two yearlings paw at a bear management "closed" (to humans) sign in Mary Bay along the Yellowstone road.

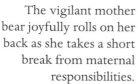

Back scratching is a common bear behavior, often learned from copying mom.

The vigilant mother bear joyfully rolls on her back as she takes a short break from maternal responsibilities.

Swimming like a furry alligator to check out a floating branch along the Brooks River shoreline.

A bear's senses are always on high gear even while resting.

The energetic cub plays with a well-worn moose antler rack along the Naknek Lake beach, Alaska.

Mom lays on her back as she and her yearling trustingly paw at each other's mouths.

and attacked me had I not stood my ground and discharged the spray when I did? Should I have sprayed when she charged the first time?

First of all, most bear charges are bluffs and I didn't want to use up the valuable spray until I deemed it absolutely necessary. Bear deterrent is most effective at close range, so while firing off a charge when a bear is thirty yards away could scare the bear off with its blasting sound, it may also do nothing more than deplete your best defensive weapon. In addition, each bear is an individual and every situation is unique. Nothing can be assumed or taken for granted.

That would certainly qualify as a surprise encounter. But the mother bear's huffing vocalizations alerted me to her presence when she was approximately fifty yards away. This gave me ample opportunity to break out the can of spray in self-defense and to prepare myself for an encounter. Its effects are temporary, so unlike a firearm properly discharged bear spray creates a win-win outcome for bear and human. At no time was I nervous, frightened, or panicked. I knew what I had to do. All was well that ended well.

This time, however, the charge was not a bluff and my bear spray did me no good. I was desperately reaching for one of the two cans that are always available in holsters on my belt, but I couldn't get to either of them. My right arm felt paralyzed, the spray canisters tantalizingly close just an inch or two away from my fingers. It was dreadfully frustrating, and I clearly realized at that moment that the difference between surviving this attack and taking my last breath might be my ability to reach and deploy that spray. I've always wanted to become one with the wilderness, but this wasn't exactly what I had in mind.

My right arm was pinned beneath me. My friend Dan Helberg, an experienced outdoorsman and chiropractor, later studied the X-rays and pieced together the likely scenario. According to Dan, the weight and strength of the mother bear, when she came charging from my right side, drove my right shoulder into the turf as I turned away from her. Her momentum was only arrested by my body's impact with the ground— much like a football linebacker buries a running back's shoulder forward and down into the turf with a vicious tackle.

Dan told me that my right shoulder apparently popped out, then back in, but the ligaments were stretched, torn, and luxated, ultimately twisting the vulnerable rotator cuff like a pretzel. At any rate, even if it had been uninjured my right arm couldn't reach my bear spray at belt level because it was pinned by her right paw. At the same time, her left front claw was raking my defenseless face at will. I felt my head crunching— *crunching!*—as I was totally at this mother grizzly bear's mercy. My right arm remained pinned underneath my body and although I never could reach the spray, I kept on trying. I had no choice; my arm was down there, and I could never have moved it back up to protect my face, for all the good it would have done.

The bear apparently also bit my left arm and raked the

back of my head with her claws as I tried to cover up and turn my face away from her. My feeling at the time was that she was purposefully tunneling her head under my body to inflict additional facial damage. The process was numbingly surreal to me; I had no idea if I was being bitten or clawed. But I do know this: if she had been biting my face with her two-inch canines instead of raking it with her curved claws, there is no way I would be alive to tell the tale. The power of a grizzly's bite is fearsome, so facial biting would have been fatal; if she had gotten my head into her jaws, she could have popped my skull like a grape. As it was, my face was as soft as modeling clay to her claws as she gave free rein to her instinct to protect her offspring at all costs.

As I found out later from the doctors in Idaho, she had literally "defaced" me, although I had no idea as to the extent of the damage at the time, which was probably a good thing. But I never fought back. Without access to my bear spray, there was little point; I would have only aggravated the bear's protective instincts by making myself more of a threat. I tried only to protect myself and certainly didn't do a very good job of that. I was completely at her mercy, a phrase that's echoed through my mind again and again since the attack.

It's that idea that I believe lies at the heart of the human fascination with and fear of the grizzly bear. We are the only animals who are aware of our own mortality, an awareness that is both blessing and curse, and that awareness lends us a profound insecurity about our vulnerability to nature's power, which remains so much greater than our own no matter what our technology makes us believe. As a result, we try to control as much about our surroundings as possible. We build cities, plow down the primeval forests and jungles and stick our animals in zoos where they are safe from us and we from them. We like to think we have control and that we're safe from nature's raw, indifferent power.

But when we confront even the idea of a grizzly bear, something primal trips in our brains. Here's an animal that is king of its environment and could easily kill an unarmed human in seconds if it chose to. When humans voluntarily venture into wild country, even with firearms, if an aggressive grizzly decides to kill and devour us, in most cases there would be virtually nothing we could do to stop it. In a way, we live and recreate in bear country at the pleasure of these mighty creatures. We are always at their mercy, and that vulnerability both transfixes and terrifies us. Though I don't share that fear, I have come to understand it.

For all I knew my life was about to end when the crunching abruptly stopped and a ghostly silence fell over the knoll. By a stroke of luck, while I lay there flattened to the earth, already completely blind in my left eye, I was somehow positioned at just the correct angle and with just enough vision in my right eye to faintly make out the blurry tail ends of a mother bear with one small cub moving away from the site. They scurried away as fast as they charged in, scrambling back toward the west.

I've rarely named bears but made an exception in this case. Over a month later, when the dust had settled, the name

"Running Bear" just came to me out of the blue. In the spirit of Native American customs and lore, this simple title seemed to make perfect sense, because the only times I briefly glimpsed the mother bear, she was running, first toward me, then away.

The silence that now lay over the knoll was eerie in comparison to the violent chaos that had gripped the scene just seconds before. It was astonishing that I could go so fast from literally fighting for my life to lying in the great quiet of Hayden Valley, listening to the trickling sounds of groundwater and of my own blood. Slowly, the stark reality of my situation washed over me: I had been spared immediate death at the claws and jaws of the mother grizzly, but I was lying alone in the middle of nowhere virtually blind and barely conscious. The mother bear had given me a chance to live, though I had no idea what was left of my head and face and never gave the matter a thought for one second. I was stunned, numb, and grateful, but I knew that living beyond the next few hours was totally up to me.

I was now alone and losing blood, very probably slipping into shock. Nobody knew where I was, because I didn't usually hike with a trail buddy and chose my route randomly. I actually wasn't more than three miles from my car as the crow flies, but no manmade trails passed through this area. I was going to have to hike myself to safety. I would have to navigate the landscape of Hayden Valley virtually sightless, injured, and weakening by the second. I'm the first to jump to a backcountry challenge, but the cold reality of this ordeal sent a chill up my spine.

All these thoughts went through my mind in a fraction of a second, in that speed-time way that things tend to happen when you've had a gallon of adrenaline dumped into your bloodstream. I had two advantages as I faced my hike out: I was in excellent physical shape, and I knew the terrain of the valley like the back of my hand. Time was my enemy, because with each passing minute I risked slipping into shock or losing enough blood to make me pass out. If I did that, I would never wake up.

My other good fortune was that the grizzly bear had never touched my legs. As I have said, I inherited powerful legs from my father, and they would be my life preservers if I was to get out of this. When attacking a human, grizzlies most commonly use their weight to overbear the person to the ground (not difficult when the bear weighs 300 pounds) and bite and claw at the head and face. The upside is that you stand a better chance of coming away with your legs unscathed, as I did and as was the case in my first mauling. They were my ticket to safety, if I could stay conscious and find my way.

From their abrupt exit, I knew that the grizzly bear family was not sticking around and no longer posed a threat. I figured I had a chance to walk out if my legs and strength held up. Again, I had no idea how badly I was injured or how much fuel was left in my tank but I knew that I was in very serious trouble. Many people have died in the wilderness of less severe injuries than mine or even from hypothermia, usually because they got hurt or lost, then panicked. I'm not a person who panics, and I knew that my mind could get me out if only my body would cooperate.

But to live, I would have to get up off the ground right that second. This was no time to rest because no one would find me in time. I needed major medical attention, pronto. Because of that, I made perhaps my most pivotal decision of that morning: I decided not to try to get out via the same route I took in. The hike around the elevated thermal area and along the ridgelines where I had surveyed the landscape for grizzlies was simply too rugged. It would surely be too much for my waning strength and the route would have been virtually impossible to find with no distinct landmark to follow. It was also riddled with steam-spewing holes that I might fall into in my sightless state.

When I hiked out after my 1993 attack, I had a rough time with the uphill portions of the trail in Glacier National Park. That was child's play compared to what I now faced with more severe injuries and no trail to follow. I had to choose the path of least resistance that would get me back to the road and within range of rescue as quickly as possible. The right strategy came into my mind instantly and without hesitation: I chose to head southeast, following the sun, and look for Trout Creek, the major landmark that would lead me to the road. It was a longer route but more navigable. That was the call of a lifetime. If I had panicked and hastily attempted to retrace my steps that day, I have no doubt I would not be alive to write this book.

I knew if I could locate Trout Creek, I could get myself to

within sight of the road. I was obviously in no shape to drive; I'd be more likely to kill myself behind the wheel than if I'd run up behind that mother grizzly and pulled on her ears. But the road, which runs over a small culvert that connects Trout Creek to the Yellowstone River, is one of the main traffic arteries through the park. There were sure to be people in the turnout, looking through binoculars for bears or just taking in the scenery. Someone would see me.

I knew my exact location. As I said, I've hiked all over Hayden Valley and intimately understood the lay of the land. I figured it was about three miles to the open flats that were in full view from the Trout Creek pullout. If I had to, I'd follow the creek right up to the road. I had no way to measure my potential endurance, but the goal was survival and this was my one and only shot. I also needed to make sure I intersected the creek at its lower course where it ran due east toward the river. If I hit it too far upstream where it turns to the south, I might become disoriented. This could significantly increase the distance I had to hike to safety, or worse, send me in the wrong direction.

With the strength left in my arms, I pushed up from the ground, rose to my feet, and then righted myself as best I could. It wasn't pretty. I was effectively blind. Only when my head was tilted way back at just the right angle, which put a strain on my neck, could I faintly see fuzzy images a few yards ahead with my right eye, which had sustained its own severe injury. The only landmark I could trust from the start was the sun. Though it was an overcast day, I could faintly recognize the sun to the southeast and I knew that it would serve as my ultimate guide. Without it, I would never have had a chance. I was like a deep-sea sailor back in the days before mechanical navigation, dependent on the heavens to find my way home.

My legs still felt relatively strong, although the attack obviously took a lot out of me. I'm sure that, just as with the attack in 1993, I was running on a heavy dose of adrenaline, and I needed to make progress before it began to wane. I began by carefully placing one wobbly foot in front of the other, one step forward at a time. My journey to survival began in earnest.

5

My Hike to Survival

Through the sagebrush valleys, through the geysers and meadows
In the deep verdant forests, they slip through the shadows
From rivers to ridge tops, this country is theirs
Bright eyed and handsome, the Yellowstone bears
Bright eyed and handsome, the Yellowstone bears
Yellowstone bears, Yellowstone bears
The most famous bears in the world

—"Yellowstone Bears," music and lyrics by James R. Cole

W HEN I WAS A child back in Chicago, my dad would sometimes lead me around the house in the dark because he wanted me to be able to find my way around when the power and lights went out during one of our infamously wicked winters. Most important, he wanted me to be comfortable with—and not afraid of—the dark. As a result, navigating by feel and instinct alone became second nature to me. Still, the challenge of keeping the couch to port and the television to starboard as an eight-year-old was nothing compared to what I faced now. I had to find my way south toward the sun, across at least two miles of sagebrush-strewn open country with no trails, and stumble across Trout Creek, which wound lazily down from Hayden Valley to the main Yellowstone road. I had to do this with virtually no eyesight, bleeding, and with unknown injuries, while slowly going into shock.

After my rescue and treatment, I would find out that in a way I had been lucky that the mother bear had injured both my eyes in the way that she did. My left eye, I would learn, had been destroyed. But my right eye was swollen shut from the sheer power of the bear's paw raking across it. My saving grace, I learned later from my surgeon, Dr. Dan Hinckley, was that her claw had cut a vertical slit in my eyelid and it was through this narrow opening that I could see the sun. I could also see the terrain downward and slightly ahead if I craned my neck, but I did not do this often because it affected my balance, and it was essential that I stay on my feet and avoid a hard fall that might worsen my injuries. Seeing the sun, however, was everything. If I had not been able to follow it, I probably would not have survived.

My other small consolation as I set out for Trout Creek was that I was sure the bear was long gone with her cub. Spooked by such close and sudden contact with a human, she had bolted and I suspected she had headed for the safety of the deep woods that surround Hayden Valley. The mother bruin had done her job: she had protected her cub from what she perceived as a threat. I wasn't worried about her in the least. I didn't give much thought to the scent of my blood drawing other predators.

I descended to the southeast down a slight grade toward a gap in the knolls that marked this part of the valley, tilting my head back periodically to track the sun. The footing seemed as good as it could be in this uneven terrain, although I didn't give it serious thought at the time. I had strong ankles and stout hiking books, but it really didn't matter. Rough or blacktop-smooth, I was going to have to hike it or die.

Three times since the attack I have hiked back to the place where I was attacked, and it seems to me now to be a perfect example of the grizzly bear's astonishing ability to blend into the landscape despite its size. The knoll I was crossing when I was mauled was small and didn't look likely to hide anything threatening. The sagebrush was scrawny and it was shocking to think it could have concealed a mammal weighing several hundred pounds. There's an old joke that sums up the impression of the scene. An artist paints a desolate desert landscape of distant buttes, a single cactus, and two rocks. He names the painting "Western Landscape with Indians." The idea is that the Indians are so good at concealment that you'll never know they're there until it's too late.

So perhaps that was the key to the attack: the bear wasn't trying to conceal herself at all. When I stumbled upon the scene—my own mistake may have been assuming that there would not be a bruin in such an unremarkable landscape—she may have seen attack as her best and only option. As I know from years of watching my beloved Chicago Bears, the best defense is a good offense. The vast majority of the time a bear encountering a human will flee the area; Running Bear may have felt that she had no such option.

The following story was told to me secondhand, but by a reliable source. A researcher was monitoring the activities of a radio-collared grizzly from a rock outcrop in Glacier National Park as the bear was foraging through vegetation near a well-used trail below. Whenever hikers came along, the bear lay down, and when they had passed, rose back up to continue foraging. This was repeated many times during the day. Apparently, no one other than the researcher saw the bear that day even though many hikers were less than fifty yards away. This is just another example of how bears avoid human contact whenever possible.

I have no doubt that a high percentage of people who hike in bear country have walked right past a bear hidden just out of sight without ever knowing it, while the bear waited patiently for them to leave the area. None of us will ever know how many bears (or other animals) we don't see because they go out of their way to avoid being seen by us. When you compare the millions of people who visit Glacier and Yellowstone each year with the microscopic number of potentially dangerous human-bear encounters, it makes you appreciate how much these creatures really want to be left alone—and to leave us alone.

What had caused my attacker to confront me? I could speculate on that later, if I was lucky. Now, I grooved myself into a steady, disciplined hiking rhythm, taking full advantage of the same all-important initial flow of adrenaline that I recalled from my 1993 mauling. My fragile body wobbled and stumbled in what I hoped was the right direction. I thought back on the attack with Tim Rubbert and asked myself, "How could this be happening to me again?" I mentally shook what was left of my head. I wondered if anyone had ever survived two grizzly maulings. I was hoping to have that dubious honor all to myself, but first I had a lot of work to do.

I remember yelling out several times, "Help me God! Please help me God!" I have never been devoutly religious, but I think the saying "no atheists in foxholes" applies here. Any and all help from any available source was welcome as I dug deep to muster up every ounce of strength. As I stumbled and fell along my rough, bushwhacking route toward the first of several small creeks, I cried a few times. But never at any point did I hesitate or lose my determination or composure. The solution to this predicament was black and white; I knew what had to be done. I kept putting one foot in front of the other.

Later, a nurse at the Idaho hospital where I was treated asked me if I had to hold my face up as I hiked out. I did not and I had never thought about it. I don't recall being that aware of the extent of my injuries. I was descending into severe shock; my exact injuries were not an issue at that point. I was fully aware that the damage was severe but I simply couldn't allow my mind to go there. If I thought about what might have been done to my body, I might panic and freeze. No negative thinking allowed.

I knew the path ahead of me and I knew that I had to avoid

the rises in the landscape if I could. I could see the sagebrush about twenty feet ahead by tilting my chin to the sky and peering through the narrow slit in my right eye, and that sliver of light kept me oriented on the sun to the southeast.

I know I didn't hold my face up because my arms were free. Having them free proved to be invaluable. Despite my injured shoulder, I pumped both arms forward and back alternately, and the swaying motion helped to build my momentum and maintain some semblance of rhythm and balance. I had to do this to compensate for the uneven terrain so that I could maintain a reasonably solid hiking pace most of the way out. I was also able to use my hands to catch myself several times when I stumbled and fell to the turf. I can only imagine the agony if I had struck my mangled head on the marshy ground.

For the next hour or so I pounded to the southeast, always keeping the sun to my right in approximately the same position. When I needed a glimpse of my whereabouts to grasp for some perspective or landmark, I would slow down and cock my head straight back. I eventually got myself into a rhythmic pattern of looking down at my feet a blurry short distance ahead and then glancing up to the right to check on the position of the sun. As long as the sun was at the correct angle, I knew I was making slow but steady progress in the right direction. No time to hesitate now. It was all or nothing. If I had miscalculated anything, like veering in the wrong direction for just a quarter or half mile, I would intersect Trout Creek at the wrong spot or miss it entirely. I knew what would happen then. Some degree of uncertainty is unavoidable at a time like this, but I knew where I was and I was confident. No other mindset was even possible. In a way, I felt lucky that if I had to be attacked, it was here in a part of the grizzly's territory that I knew like my old suburban Chicago neighborhood. If I had been mauled in a place with which I had been less familiar, without a trail to follow, this story may have had a different outcome.

My strategy was simple: take the path of least topographic resistance to a landmark that I knew I wouldn't need my eyes to follow. If I could locate Trout Creek, I could follow its rushing sound and give my traumatized eye and head a break. In theory, that is. I had no choice but to climb a small rise that I would have galloped up in seconds when my body was sound. Now, it took almost all the energy I had left. But I knew that I was in the section of the valley carved out by the creek's loops and winds. If I didn't lose my way over the last half mile, I would soon hit the creek and be one step closer to getting out of this mess.

I covered the last few hundred yards in my lurching, unsteady gait and then I heard it: the applause sound of rushing water. There was no other stream in the area that had that volume of water, so I knew I had found Trout Creek. I had been confident about locating it, but actually finding the creek gave me a new shot of adrenaline that restored my flagging energy. However, this was no time to rest on my laurels. I knew that I still had at least a mile to go, following the creek downstream toward the road. From that point forward, though my proximity to it varied with the difficulty of the terrain and the hardship of crossing the water, I clung to the creek like a lover.

Turning due east as best I could, I continued to bulldoze

forward. I was feeling better about things now; as long as I kept contact with the creek, I knew that eventually I would reach the open country in view of the Trout Creek turnout. There were always people there glassing for grizzlies or bison and the odds were good that someone would see me. The issue now was endurance. I had to conserve enough strength to trudge along the creek and make it to the open flats.

During some stretches, I attempted to travel the high flat banks through the dry sagebrush where the footing was good, but I was also trying to avoid making any significant energy-draining elevation changes unless I had no choice. Trout Creek is laced with sharp, meandering switchback-like curves that often turn on a dime like a downhill Olympic ski run. The effect is charming when you're wandering aimlessly with perfect health and all the time in the world, but it presented me with a problem. The creek turns (some actually curving back in the opposite direction) are so severe that a strategy of strictly following along the creek bank would have doubled or tripled my walking distance at a part of my journey when I could not afford to waste a single calorie of energy. On the other hand, if I left the creek and guessed at its route to bypass the radical switchbacks, I might lose the creek altogether.

Faced with choosing A or B, I selected C. I would make my own path by fording the stream where it seemed to be safe to cross. This would allow me the best of both worlds (or perhaps the least bad of two bad options): I could stick to the creek without wasting precious energy tracing every twist and turn. Thanks to my years of experience in this country, I was able to find easy crossing routes fairly quickly. Short crossings usually indicate deep water, because the swiftness of the current cuts a deep crevice in the earth, so I tried to pick out the accessible wide spots without having to veer far off course. I was able to maintain my wobbly balance during at least five separate crossings. In reality, I lost count of how many times I crossed. I only know that I was determined not to let the creek pass from my hearing and that I would keep going no matter how wet I got. My camera holster remained relatively dry so I must have done a good job.

My vision never changed. When I cocked my head back like a man in a dentist's chair, I still saw only an indistinct version of my legs and feet and a little of the terrain a short distance in front of me. Everything else was dark except for the reassuring presence of the sun. I yelled out at the top of my lungs for help a couple of times (as if someone would actually be in earshot; hardly any tourists ever hike into Hayden Valley) but the best I could do was pathetically weak with almost no volume, so I decided not to expend the energy. One foot in front of the other was my priority.

I remember slipping and sliding up a muddy creek bank and stopping to catch my breath at the top. It seemed like Mt. Everest. I recalled how difficult the uphill stretches were when I hiked out from Fifty Mountain with Tim Rubbert in 1993. I stopped at the top for about thirty seconds to catch my breath, one of only about three or four brief breaks I allowed myself. Momentum was everything. I knew I was getting colder and I dreaded stiffening up or slipping into hypothermia. I took deep, deep breaths. I couldn't see my watch, if I still had it, but I knew I was running out of time. The tight switchbacks were sapping more and more of my strength.

I suppose in such a situation it's natural to think about death and life. As you've discovered, I'm a very emotional man when it comes to the people in my life, and I certainly had plenty of emotional memories of them all. My reflections at the time were that if this was to be the end, it had been a great life. No regrets. Plenty of mistakes, but no regrets. Believe it or not, I really don't regret anything that I have ever done because, given the circumstances and my life experiences, I probably would have done most everything the same way. Looking back in an attempt to learn from my numerous mistakes has been a worthwhile exercise throughout my life, but I've never second-guessed myself because I have always felt guided by my passion.

Surprisingly, as I stumbled through the brush in a desperate attempt to escape death, I felt a wave of profound gratitude and peace of mind. My heart filled with appreciation and a sense of the good fortune I had experienced—discovering my passion for grizzlies and the wilderness and actually living out my dreams like very few humans have. What a gift! My passion for life came from my dad, who lived out his own dreams. They were very different dreams from mine, but that doesn't matter. It's the pursuit that counts, not the specifics.

My adventures have taken me to prime grizzly habitat eighteen times in Alaska, along with thousands of miles in grizzly country in the Lower 48. While I was on the ultimate hike for my life, I knew that there were a lot of new adventures in store for me. I didn't want to miss them. I wasn't about to be forced into premature retirement if I had anything to say about it. It has always been my mission to get out there and educate the public about grizzly bears, and mountains of work lay ahead to serve that mission. This period in my life was supposed to be the beginning of a new era when my longtime field labors would bear fruit through my teaching others the incredible truth about *Ursus arctos*.

What's more, I have been blessed with wonderful family and friends throughout my life. This was way too soon to check out on them. My sister Tootsie's children, Cara and Jeff, have been deserted at just about every turn and I needed to be there for them. My pal Ron, who you'll meet shortly, had two daughters who were pregnant for the first time and I had to live long enough to see him as a proud grandfather. My death at this time would affect so many lives. I had to survive for them, as well as for myself.

My thoughts wandered to *It's a Wonderful Life* starring James Stewart. One of the themes of this Frank Capra classic is that the impact we have on the lives of others is never truly appreciated until we're gone. Like George Bailey, I did have a choice out there in Hayden Valley. I could have lain down and fallen asleep and spared myself the pain to come, just as Jimmy Stewart's character could have jumped off that bridge into the icy river. But I chose life over death. Life is just too damned interesting to check out before closing time.

To this day—and I don't mean this to sound egotistical—I still half cannot believe that I did what I did. If you'd written it as a Hollywood screenplay, every producer in town would dismiss it as being unrealistic. But when I look at the combination of everything—my injuries, the distance I had to travel, the trauma to my body, the fact that I could hardly see, no trail to follow—it still seems half unreal. What made me able to keep my cool, focus my mind, keep my body from collapsing, and get to the road? I still don't really know how I did it and I probably never will.

Not until I finally reached Trout Creek did I know that I could make it out. I still had a long way to go from that point, but once I found the creek, I felt positive I would reach the park road. I had a vision of the culvert where Trout Creek runs under the road and flows into the Yellowstone River. I would make for that culvert. In my mind's eye, I developed tunnel vision. Survival was the only acceptable outcome and, unbeknownst to me, the folks who would help me survive were on their way.

Judy and John Taylor were casually driving north through Hayden Valley when, on a moment's impulse, they decided to "pull off at the last second" at Trout Creek to view wildlife in Hayden Valley. They live in Pocatello, Idaho, a few hours away, and go to the park whenever they can. John, an avid fly fisherman, is a big outdoor enthusiast in general and Judy's interests matched his. This day, they pulled to the roadside and were intently glassing with binoculars for bears when Judy first spotted me, probably close to a half mile away.

John noticed a sling pack on my hip and reasoned that I might be a research biologist carrying equipment to take samples. Judy thought I was wearing a facemask to protect my face; John would later call it a "neoprene camouflage face mask." Later, he would share the chilling information that at least two coyotes had been circling me as I walked toward the road. The crafty canines obviously smelled my blood and were waiting for me to take a final fall before moving in. A healthy adult male human is too much for even a small pack of coyotes, but I was hardly healthy and if I'd gone down, they might have had one hell of a feast. Sorry to disappoint you, guys.

Judy told me later, "We'd see you, then you'd drop out of sight. It happened again, then again, and then again. We were still looking for animals when you got closer, limping or dragging a foot, basically walking along the creek. You seemed to be aimlessly wandering, not walking straight lines. We thought you might be handicapped or drunk."

It turned out that my recollection, which is understandably fuzzy, was not entirely accurate. Early on in the hike I was fording the creek when I could to avoid the switchbacks but later it seems that I was following the winding course of the streambed as it switched back on itself. I'm sure I did this because descending and then climbing the banks of Trout Creek was simply too much for me, but following the creek's loops at this point gave me the security of knowing that I was following the correct route near the finish line. It also added

139

distance to my walk and wore me down, but that seemed to be the lesser of two evils. No doubt that meandering path, along with my unsteady and weakening legs, convinced Judy that perhaps I was either crazy or had been hitting the bottle in the backcountry.

John and Judy monitored my slow progress along the creek for twenty to thirty minutes before they realized something was seriously wrong. By this time, I could hear the cars passing on the road and I knew I was near to rescue. I would not die alone in the wilderness and be eaten by wolves. It was a good thing, because my strength was just about spent. I was on the south side of Trout Creek, close to the culvert where creek meets river, and about fifty yards from the road when John came out to get me.

"I saw him sitting on the bank about fifty yards from the road," John said in a later interview with Tim Vandehey. "I just looked through my binoculars and realized his face was covered with blood." John told me later that he knew right then that I had been mauled by a bear. He immediately came out to render assistance. My only memory of those last few seconds of my long journey to the road are John's voice and seeing a hazy human figure that I hoped wasn't a hallucination. I said to John, "Help, I got attacked by a bear." As he said, "Yeah, I can see that," I collapsed in his arms as he caught me. A feeling of safety and security came over me. I was utterly spent, but I had done my job. I had hiked into Hayden Valley at about 8:30 that morning. It was about 1:00 in the afternoon when I reached the road.

For the three days after that moment, I have no memory. I

have reconstructed the rest based on the testimony of others who were at the scene. "I was amazed you had the strength to walk across the creek," John told me later. Judy maintained that while I was being given emergency aid, my voice remained calm throughout as I matter-of-factly told John what happened.

Judy later related that she had "a weird feeling in the pit of [her] stomach" as she cleaned out the back seat of their car to make room to drive me to the nearest hospital. However, due to the severity of my injuries, it immediately became evident that the best course of action was to wait for an ambulance. There was no way my trauma could have been properly treated at the medical facilities in Yellowstone.

According to Judy, I was shivering; the temperature hovered around freezing and I had lost a lot of blood. "John carried and hand-dragged you over onto the embankment about twenty feet from the road," she said. "You had no ear, no nose, no eye, no cheek. Everything was gone and hanging down. It reminded me of a Hollywood horror movie costume."

"You were quite a sight to see," said John. "I've thought about it a lot, but no nightmares. I could see the path of the claw marks from the base of the neck to the hairline right through the face, eyes, and nose: four claws. You didn't have a face. You were a bloody mess. It reminded me of the Michael Jackson 'Thriller' video, the way zombies were dancing around."

"When you declared, 'I'm hypothermic,' we took the liners out of both of our coats and an elderly couple stopped with a space blanket," Judy added. "Cars were starting to slow and stop to see what was going on, which I find amusing now."

Judy stood in the road and told curiosity seekers to keep going while John stayed with me and sopped up blood with rolls of paper towels. In spite of being dropped into such a gruesome scene without warning, they handled the situation well, which surprises them to this day. "We were both amazingly calm," Judy said.

On May 1, 2008, I finally reconnected with the Taylors for the first time since they had rescued me from my lurching death march through Hayden Valley. It was an emotional time for all of us, revealing and valuable, because they filled in a lot of blanks for me . . . and I filled in a few for them. Hearing each other's voices and recounting the events together for the first time was an intense and humbling way to spend a Thursday afternoon.

Judy told me that their original plan for their trip was to drive through Hayden Valley on Tuesday, but that those plans had to be scrapped when they got wind of a storm on its way to West Yellowstone. So they reevaluated their plans. Instead of Hayden Valley on Tuesday, they planned to visit Lamar Valley (a very popular wildlife viewing spot in the park) on Tuesday, then go into the town of Cody. That would put them in Hayden on May 23rd, fortunately for me. In fact, some odd things happened with John and Judy that give my relationship with them a very meant-to-be quality.

On the day that they found me, they had been sightseeing at a nearby mountain that was a steep climb for them. But help was on the way. "A man in a golf cart asked us if we needed a lift to the top, and we said sure," Judy said. "He didn't give anyone else a ride, and when we were done he offered us a ride down. But when we went to look for him, he had disappeared. If we hadn't saved all that time riding up and down, we might not have been at Trout Creek in time to spot you."

It was refreshing to discover that I was rescued by folks who have a sound comfort level with grizzlies. Understandably, they were both initially a little more nervous about camping after seeing what happened to me, but ultimately their attitudes remain unchanged. John speaks for them both when he says: "If you're careful, it's okay to be in grizzly country."

During our reunion, John also said, "I'm thankful I was there to help you and I'm glad you survived. This changes a person. We're proud of how we handled it. The angels were looking out for you."

No, John. You and Judy were looking out for me. You and some guy with a golf cart.

At that same time, Judy Geiger and her parents were enjoying their annual family pilgrimage to the park and cruising north along the Grand Loop Road through Hayden Valley at just after 1:00. They planned on hiking the trail near the brink of Yellowstone Falls followed by a leisurely lunch, but you know what they say about best laid plans.

Judy Geiger was driving as they slowly passed the gathering near Trout Creek. She estimates that it was about five minutes after the Taylors found me. When she saw me covered in blood, her first impression was that I might have been gored by a bison or in an automobile accident. "It didn't even dawn on me that it would have been a bear," she said. "I don't know why it didn't dawn on me, it just didn't." The reality of the matter is that far more visitors are injured by bison than bears in Yellowstone, and auto accidents are common, so Judy's initial reaction was common sense.

Judy threw her Saturn Vue into a U-turn and returned to the scene. She walked up to the Taylors, who were administering first aid. "I'm a nurse. Do you need some help?" she said. They responded, "Please stay."

Judy Geiger was the nursing director of the Pediatric Intensive Care Unit at Primary Children's Medical Center in Salt Lake City, Utah. She's been a nurse for twenty-five years, the past nineteen in pediatric intensive care. But even with all that experience, "I was really shocked," she said. "I'd seen a lot of gory injuries but this was pretty gross. When I first saw you, it looked like you had a bloody bandana over your face. It was shocking! I could tell where your eyes should be but could not locate them and I wasn't about to go probing around."

In a later interview for KSL television station in Salt Lake City, Judy said, I really couldn't tell at the time when I saw him whether he still had eyes because things were sort of rearranged and bloody. His face was just hanging off, basically. I was sort of shocked that he could have walked three miles back from where he was hurt. I really think if he had not been going in the right direction or this couple hadn't seen him and he'd fallen down and for some reason couldn't get back up, I think he could have died. She has continually insisted that, "the people who found you did the most."

Her parents had a first aid kit in their car containing much-needed gloves and bandages. Judy Geiger went to work with these while Judy Taylor, with John's help, tried to prevent a traffic jam from clogging up the scene and preventing emergency vehicles from reaching me. But they needed some help. Fortunately, six to twelve people took it upon themselves to assist the Taylors in directing traffic and together they successfully kept the cars moving for the most part, preventing the crowd from turning into a "Jim jam."

Meanwhile, I was in bad shape. The entire left side of my face was hanging down from my skull in a way that almost looked comically exaggerated, exactly as John described—like the "Thriller" video. Looking back at the photos taken by the Park Service (photos so gruesome I have hardly shown them to anyone), it is hard to believe that anyone could suffer an injury like mine and live. But amazingly, I was able to breathe, move, and think, so it was plain that it actually could have been much, much worse.

Judy Geiger began treating my facial injury by "holding it on, putting pressure on the bleeding with one of the bandages," she said. "I didn't know how to describe how it was; it was as if the bear took it off in the one big piece that was hanging. Then there was the three to three-and-a-half-inch gash on your head that still bled a little." She noted that the majority of my bleeding had already taken place on the walk out. She asked me my name and if I could breathe okay. I told her my name and then said that I wasn't having trouble breathing.

She was surprised. Later, she said, "I thought your airway might be compromised, and that you were lucky not to be choking on your own blood, not to put too fine a point on it." But she quickly realized that if I had been able to walk out an unknown distance on my own, I was probably not having trouble breathing.

She asked if I was hurt anywhere else. "No, all in my head and face," I replied. She explained to me what was going on as I kept asking when the Emergency Medical Technicians (EMTs) would arrive. I told Judy that I was "cold and hurting" as my body shivered badly. I was slipping into shock. One person at the scene brought out a solar blanket and numerous folks took off their coats and threw them on me.

Judy noted that I was hypothermic and that the pulse on my wrist was "very weak, but there." She thought I must have been in severe pain and she wanted to stay close so she could continue to hold my face on, make sure I had an airway, and be certain that I continued to breathe. My body was now fighting a substantial loss of body heat and blood, and with my adrenaline rush gone, I was also losing the battle against lethargy and shock. She said I was fairly quiet as she answered my questions. She knew I was all right as long as I kept talking, which I apparently did. Even a grizzly attack can't shut me up. She repeated, "You're doing okay. They are coming!"

Later, Judy shared a cute story from that fateful time. She noticed that a Park Service water truck had pulled over. The driver got out and said, "Oh, I'm worried about where the bear is." The idea that this incident occurred far from the road apparently never occurred to him. Judy said that I immediately blurted out, "Oh no! Don't worry. I walked out three miles back."

Judy Geiger took excellent care of me while the EMTs were summoned. She informed me the moment that the ambulance sirens faintly sounded in the distance.

U.S. Park Ranger Rick Fey arrived on the scene within ten minutes of my rescue. This material appears in his official report:

I asked the person to his left, also sitting down, who was applying pressure to his chin if she was involved in this incident. She responded "No, but I'm a nurse." I thanked her for her assistance and asked that she continue giving him support. His nose and nasal cavity appeared to be gone, so was his mandible and most of the soft tissue around it. It appeared that his eyes were missing. It was difficult for me to recognize facial landmarks. I recognized his eyebrows. Everything below that was unrecognizable. Even though it appeared that he was supporting himself, I could not believe that his airway was not compromised. I could not figure out how this individual was able to breathe!

I asked the patient his name. He tried to answer me but I could not understand him. His answers were garbled. I asked him again and this time he told me Jim Cole. It sounded that his tongue was also missing, it was apparent that his jaw was. I continued to access his mental and breathing status by asking questions. I asked him, "Where did this happen?" (about two to three miles behind me to the west) "How many others are out there?" (none, I was by myself) "What did this to you?" (a grizzly with a cub) "When did this happen?" We paused. I told him it was now 1:00 o'clock, how many hours ago did this happen? (about two hours ago, around 11:00)

I asked, "Whose stuff is this?" Someone said it was the patient's. It was in its own pile not far from the scene. I noticed blood on several of the items, especially one of the two bear sprays. However, the camera seemed to me to be surprisingly clear of blood. I asked the patient if this was his stuff. (Yes) I immediately seized the camera and put it in my patrol car.

Finally, about fifteen minutes after the Taylors had pulled me up the embankment to the road, the ambulance and EMTs arrived. Upon arrival, an EMT cut off the black fleece jacket that had kept me warm out in the wilderness for the past sixteen years. It was my favorite hiking garment for any kind of cool to bitterly cold weather. I would often wear it with layers and I had acquired it on sale in Ely, Minnesota, in March 1991—my first year out in the field full-time. Easy come easy go, I guess. Call me a sentimental slob but I miss that jacket.

The next step was to get life-sustaining fluids into my injury-riddled body to combat the shock and loss of blood. With Judy's help, the EMT inserted an IV of vital fluids and electrolytes into the big vein on the inside of my elbow. Judy Geiger's final act was to help the three-person EMT team load me into the ambulance. I didn't hear a word from the Taylors again until nearly a year later, and only thanks to a strange coincidence.

U.S. Park Ranger Laura Anderson wrote in her report:

I transported Cole to West Yellowstone Clinic on MS-81 with Ranger Lojko and paramedic Mitch Copeland. During the transport, I questioned Cole as to what happened. Cole stated that the bear surprised him and he surprised the bear, and the attack happened very quickly. I asked Cole if he had any pictures on his camera of that particular sow and cub, and he stated that he did not.

Right now, speed was of the essence. I clearly needed a fully equipped trauma center. The decisions were out of my hands as I sped toward West Yellowstone and an uncertain future.

6

Eastern Idaho Regional Medical Center

Cause he's the funny man
But he doesn't try to be that way
He's just such a jolly fellow and I dare you all to stay
He'll have you laughing from the inside
Like a dog scratching fleas
And when you're all laughed out after a while
He'll quickly turn around and smile
And put you back down on your knees

—"Funny Man," music and lyrics by James R. Cole

I WAS TAKEN JUST under fifty road miles by ambulance on the Northern Grand Loop route through Canyon, Norris, and Madison junctions to West Yellowstone, a small tourist border town at the western entrance and boundary of Yellowstone Park. From there, a Flight for Life helicopter with a crew of three airlifted me to the landing pad right in front of the Eastern Idaho Regional Medical Center (EIRMC) Emergency Room.

I wondered for some time why the Park Service didn't have

a helicopter fly directly to the turnout where I was receiving first aid and pick me up there, shaving ninety minutes off the time I could get to a hospital. Later, I found out from the Official Park Service Incident Record that a Medical Helicopter had been immediately requested to the scene with an ETA of fifty minutes. However, rangers on the scene decided that I would be taken to West Yellowstone in an ambulance and meet the helicopter there.

Mind you, I have no memory of my ambulance ride or of my subsequent flight into eastern Idaho. I'm reconstructing all of this from many interviews with the people involved. I'm a little disappointed that I wasn't conscious to enjoy flying so low over such beautiful country, but we weren't on a sightseeing trip. The only mission was to get me to a functioning ER and into the hands of a trauma team to make sure that I would survive my injuries.

At EIRMC I was greeted by an awaiting trauma team composed of about twenty hospital personnel including a trauma surgeon, ER doctor, two ER nurses, an ICU nurse, a recorder, and many others. Of course, I was unconscious for this entire process and missed all the excitement. But in light of my subsequent visits to Idaho Falls, I can really picture the scene in my mind. EIRMC is a complex of red brick buildings on the edge of Idaho Falls, near new housing developments, and it towers above everything else around it. Everything in the ER is state of the art, and because of their proximity to Yellowstone as well as Grand Teton National Park, the staff is experienced at dealing with animal maulings. I was, as I would find out later, in the best of hands.

Fortunately for me, two of those hands belonged to Dr. Dan Hinckley, a celebrated ear, nose, and throat surgeon who is truly beloved by the people at EIRMC. I saw this many times upon my return visits: when I spoke about Dan to the nurses and staff, their faces would light up. This doesn't happen when you mention a lot of doctors; it happened all the time with Dan Hinckley.

Dan is a kind, soft-spoken Mormon who lives with his large family in a gorgeous house in the hills above rural Idaho Falls, and when he's not practicing medicine he's raising miniature horses. He possesses the quality that I think is most vital in a great doctor: an unshakable calm. He's also become a close and dear friend. I had fallen, by sheer good luck, into the care of an extraordinary physician.

EIRMC gets two to three maulings every one to two years from the entire region, and it didn't take Dr. Hinckley long to see that my case was as severe as a mauling can be and leave the patient alive. He and his team assessed that my airway was open and I was getting oxygen and that my other vital functions were relatively stable. Obviously, since I had hiked out for three miles after the injury, I was in better shape than I might otherwise have been. But my survival was hardly a sure thing. My face was devastated. My left eye was probably a total loss. My nose, left cheekbone, and other facial bones were shattered and splintered. The foundation of bone on which a human face is stretched was basically gone. The task at hand was simple yet overwhelming: reconstruct my face from eyebrows to mouth with nothing to go on, not even a driver's license picture. My ID was back in my van, which had been impounded by the Park Service.

Time was of the essence, in part because of the great risk of infection, but a big decision had to be made right away. Either Dr. Hinckley and his team would perform this complicated procedure at EIRMC or ship me off to a Salt Lake City hospital. Dr. Hinckley carefully assessed the injuries. "You look for things you can't do or haven't done before," he said later.

Dan had total confidence in his abilities and felt that he was the best person for the job. He had first-hand experience sewing up bear mauling victims, while in Salt Lake City there was no way of knowing whether I would get a surgeon with animal attack experience or just the surgeon in residence at the time I arrived. So the decision was made and into surgery I went. Dan was supported by Dr. Catherine Durborow, who did an extraordinary job of reconstructing my right eyelid, a vital component of this bloody mess. Jointly they went to work putting Humpty Dumpty back together.

At some point either in the ambulance, the helicopter, or at the hospital, I must have told someone Richard Berman's name and phone number. The Taylors and Judy Geiger concurred that I had not given out that piece of information prior to departing in the ambulance, so this curious detail remains a mystery. But without identification, there was no way for hospital personnel to notify anyone who might be able to support me during my stay. Piecing things together from the accounts of nurses and staff, I concluded that while I was semi-conscious, someone asked me if there was anyone they could call, and I said, "my brother," referring to Richard Berman. If anyone would drop everything to be by my side, it would be him.

A routine Wednesday afternoon was coming to an end for Richard at "Rich's Tennis School," an indoor facility located about twelve miles east of Boulder. Richard has been a professional tennis instructor since the early 1970s and has become one of the finest in the country. He is also one of the top wheelchair tennis coaches in the world. His prize student, Australian David Hall, won an Olympic gold medal and seven U.S. Open titles and was ranked number one in the world for close to seven years. Most exceptionally, Richard has never accepted any payment from David. He is my best friend and true soul brother.

At 4:30 P.M., he was working with a fifteen-year-old female student while her mother attentively looked on when the telephone rang. Richard rarely responds to calls during lessons, but the ringing didn't stop, so he finally interrupted the lesson and reluctantly answered.

After Richard picked up the phone and began to listen, he at first thought that this blatant interruption was nothing more than a bothersome telemarketer. The lady on the other end of the phone gave her name, Linda Harwell, repeated it a couple of times, and said that she was a social worker from the

Eastern Idaho Regional Medical Center. She asked if his name was Richard Cole.

He said, "No, please tell me again who is calling." Linda repeated her name and again said she was calling from EIRMC. Richard said, "You must have the wrong number because I don't know anyone from Idaho."

Linda pleaded with Richard not to hang up so he finally asked, "What does this pertain to?" She told him that there had been a serious bear mauling and Richard suddenly knew, to his horror, what the call was about.

He said, "Oh my God! I know who you are talking about. My name is Rich Berman."

Linda asked, "Are you Jim Cole's brother?"

Richard answered, "I am like his brother. We've been best friends for close to forty years, but please write down that I am his brother. How serious is it?"

"How quickly can you get here?" she said.

"Is there any fear that Jim will not survive?" he asked.

"We don't know."

Linda gave Richard all the information he would need, including her phone number and the emergency room phone number at the hospital. Richard said, "I have no idea where you are but I will be there as soon as I can," and hung up.

I can't imagine ever getting a call like that. Richard told me later that he was deeply shaken by it. "When it first sunk in—my closest friend, Jim Cole, has been mauled, and the people at the hospital couldn't tell me whether he would survive or not—it was a panic," Richard said. "I didn't even know where Idaho Falls was." He turned to his assistant, Alan Tsuda, and said, "I'm leaving now for an emergency and I don't know when I'll be back. I know you'll take care of everything."

Richard jumped in his car, headed for home, and immediately called his son Bret, who is very Internet-savvy. "Son, get me to Idaho Falls as fast as you can," he said. The quickest travel scenario Bret could piece together was for his dad to catch an evening flight to Salt Lake City, rent a car, then drive the 210 miles to Idaho Falls. Richard thought, "What kind of doctor is he going to get out in potato country?"

The phone rang at Richard's house as he was preparing to leave for the Denver airport. It was Dr. Hinckley, who was about to begin the hours-long task of putting my face back together. Richard's first response was, "Doctor, you ask the questions." Dr. Hinckley wanted to know if Richard was familiar with my medical history, if I was allergic to anything, and what drugs I was taking. Richard was able to answer most of the doctor's questions, partly because he had been with me a month earlier during a heart ablation procedure in Billings, Montana. He told Dr. Hinckley everything he could, and then he was out the door headed for Denver International Airport, talking to his son on the phone as he drove to get instructions.

"I asked Dr. Hinckley, 'Will he live?' and he told me he didn't know," Richard said later. "As I'm driving from Salt Lake to Idaho Falls, there was an emergency nurse who I was in contact with every hour and a half or so. But there weren't many updates because the surgery was eight or nine hours long."

By the time Richard arrived at EIRMC many hours later, I had just gotten out of nine hours-plus of surgery. A titanium substructure was now holding my face together, my right eye was saved, and my nose was detached from the facial bones due to a compound fracture. The bear had clawed me to the skull, back to front, then right to left. This was only the first of many surgeries that I would require.

As friends will, many of my friends have taken full advantage of my woes by remarking that any new face could only be a significant improvement. I guess that's what friends are for. When I was coherent enough to appreciate it, I actually enjoyed this sarcastic humor; it was a tacit way of saying that everything was going to be all right. In fact, without the humor as well as the love and support of my friends during those early days in the EIRMC, I think my chances of a full recovery would have been far slimmer.

All in all, I'd say I look pretty good today when you consider the trauma inflicted on my face. My left eye was a lost cause; when I'm not around friends or family I wear an eye patch to keep from drawing stares. The patch draws stares in itself but is a better alternative. But other than a prominent scar high on my left cheekbone from the surgery to reconstruct my face and a now-covered bald spot that Dr. Hinckley says was caused by a claw raking my head, I don't think I look too bad. Again, my friends reading this will probably disagree and claim that I'm better looking now than before the mauling. Most important, I can see out of my right eye, drive, read, think, and enjoy life.

I did not look anything remotely resembling good when Richard first walked into Intensive Care Unit room 217 shortly after my long surgery. He had spent many hours alone on the road trying to keep his brain from taking him to the darkest places. "The whole time out there, I wouldn't allow my mind to go where it wanted to go, which was, 'When I arrive, what the hell am I going to do if he's dead?'" he said to Tim later. "The box I put my mind in was, get the hell to Idaho Falls safely. There were deer on the road so I couldn't even drive the speed limit."

When a security guard, also named Richard, walked him to my room, what he saw in this compact space directly across from the nurses' station was a bedridden figure that "didn't look human. I was totally shocked!" He confided to me a couple of months later that nausea quickly set in and he almost threw up the Burger King burger he'd grabbed in Pocatello during his mad rush to get to Idaho Falls.

Suppressing his desire to vomit, he turned to the security guard. "You've made a mistake, this isn't my brother at all. Take me to the right room," he said. The security guard grabbed Richard by the shoulder and said, "This is your brother, that's Jim." My face was so torn up, bloodied, stitched, and stapled together that my best friend absolutely did not recognize me, though he knew my mug like the back of his hand.

"I almost collapsed, got weak-kneed, and almost fell backward," Richard says. "It took me about twenty seconds and then I got my composure and really looked. Jim looked like a bowling ball. The swelling was grotesque. The holes where the fingers would go were his eyes, the hole where the thumb would go was his mouth. The intensive care nurse I first met on duty told me, "We don't know if he is going to survive." It was too soon to tell, she said. That, I have found, is the mantra of most medical personnel: give hope but not false hope. Don't overpromise. They would do the best they could for me but the rest was up to me. Fortunately, I'm a stubborn son of a bitch.

As Richard continued to look down at my mangled figure on the bed, connected to a myriad of tubes and monitors leading in and out of my body while a ventilator handled my breathing and a tube fed me, he accepted the hard fact that this actually was me. He took a deep breath and his composure returned right away, like I always knew it would in the face of a crisis. He confided to me that it took two full days before he personally felt confident that I would actually make it through this ordeal. "Your survival was a hell of a birthday gift," he told me. Richard's birthday was also the first day I started on the long and unpredictable road to recovery.

EIRMC was nice enough to give my "brother" a room with a shower. All he did was walk in, drop off some personal belongings, turn around, and immediately return to my ICU bedside for the beginning of a long vigil. I have to say here that the kindness of the hospital staff was incredible throughout my contact with them. I have serious doubts that I and my friends would have received the same kind of personal, caring, above-and-beyond-the-call attention from the people at a busy big city hospital. Not to say that people in an ICU in New York or Los Angeles aren't as dedicated as those in eastern Idaho, but they are simply busier and more stressed out and dealing with things like drug overdoses and gang shootings. The doctors, nurses, and other people at EIRMC were, to a man and woman, amazing. I am deeply in their debt.

Later that morning, a sleep-deprived Richard received a call from Ron Giangiorgi, my other great friend, an attorney who is also known as "Buster Brown," "The Vulture," "Opossum," "The Gumper," and "Bagelman." "I was at work, and really found out about the attack by accident," Ron told Tim. "My brother, who was in semi-retirement, was at home that morning, and he's an Internet news buff. My wife was on the phone with my sister-in-law and she heard in the background my brother saying, 'Oh my God, Jim got attacked again.'

"She got as many details as she could from the article," Ron continued. "She picked up the phone and called me at work. I was surprised, because normally I'm one of the first folks to get called when something happens. I have Jim programmed into my cell phone, so I punched him in and got nothing, which isn't unusual—he's often out in areas with no cell service. Then I called him at home, got his wife, and she told me he was at the hospital. I called the hospital and of course they won't give out any information; in fact, they had him there under a different name."

Hospital staff told Ron that my brother was at the hospital, and since Ron knew I didn't have a biological brother, it had to be Richard. He called Richard, who explained the situation and told him the extent of my injuries. Richard told Ron not to come; it was just too gruesome. "Bullshit," said Ron. "I'm coming. Where are you?" Ron called his wife, Loretta, back and said, "Get me on a plane to Idaho Falls as soon as possible. I don't care what it costs." He was in my room within two days of the attack.

Ron is an animated, colorful, humorous character with impeccable common sense. We've been the closest of friends since high school in Highland Park, Illinois. He had been my battery mate and pitching protégé during our days playing twelve-inch fast-pitch softball, and earned the nickname "The Vulture" (after Cubs reliever Phil Regan) after coming into a game as a relief pitcher and earning the only save in team history. If Richard is brother number one, Ron is my second brother.

He is also a former certified EMT and volunteer fireman, so he's no stranger to injuries. As a fireman, following in his father's footsteps in his hometown of Highwood, Illinois, he brought three people back from the brink of death with CPR. Years later, after Ron became a lawyer, a man was having a seizure during a business meeting and was choking on his own blood. While others around him panicked, Ron simply, calmly rolled the guy over on his side until the seizure passed. He was rewarded with two tickets to the second night game ever played in Wrigley Field.

Ironically, Ron suffers from ischemic optic neuropathy. This causes random blind spots in his right center field of vision in addition to significantly reduced peripheral vision in both eyes. He can still legally drive a motorized vehicle, but his safety concerns for others outweigh any benefits so Ron has voluntarily suspended all driving. I've never once heard him grumble about this. We now joke that between us, we possess a grand total of two good eyes.

Ron made one request of Richard before departing the Windy City. "If Jim wakes up before I get there," he said, "tell him two-fifty." Richard had no idea what this meant but said he would do it. Two-fifty is the required opening bid for the player receiving the deal in a unique two-handed pinochle game Ron and I have played together for close to forty years. We play every chance we get and we're both fiercely competitive.

Ron explained to Tim later, "We play it with my family around and spend a lot of time playing this game. Once we were in a small town near Yellowstone, and we went into this hotel to eat dinner. Afterward, we sat in the bar and played this game. People watched us play because we were so intense about it even though we have never played for money. Richard and I would talk about this to Jim when he was coming around after he was under pain medication; it calmed him down."

Ron arrived from Chicago (via Phoenix and Boise) on Friday morning. When he got to the hospital, he was promptly informed that there was no James Cole there. The hospital had given me a fake name to shield me from the media. But Richard received a message that Ron had arrived and came down to greet him. My two lifelong pals had previously only known each other from one dinner at Richard's old house in Boulder many years ago, and at my wedding and bachelor party. Now they would be seeing a whole lot of each other over the next week and a half. I can only imagine what they talked about those first few days.

Richard had begun keeping a journal about my recovery. One journal entry read, "I'm so pleased the swelling is down and Ron will be able to distinguish you from that bowling ball I saw yesterday." However, Ron still barely recognized me. But he was finally able to discern my features through the bloody mess. He had brought along a black Chicago White Sox flag and one of the first things he did was clip it to my bed. This sniff of familiarity, although I could not actually see the flag, became a fixture during my stay in Idaho and now hangs in my office in a place of honor.

Under heavy sedation, I slept through that entire first full day in the hospital, Thursday, May 24th. Other friends wanted to come out to Idaho Falls and I really appreciated those heartfelt offers. Richard and Ron became my watchdogs: they rotated through my room 24/7, watched me so they could report any changes to the ICU nurses or doctors on rounds, and acted as my gatekeepers, taking calls from other concerned friends and fending off unwanted attention. They became bosom friends with the people who ran the hospital's Subway concession. Though I didn't know it as I unconsciously fought for my life, my "A" team was in place. These two are like brothers to me and they were both there with me every step of my road back to life.

Through all of this, I was also in the throes of a divorce. My soon-to-be ex-wife wanted to exert control by coming to the hospital. Richard and Ron knew that she would only cause stress and aggravation and was the last person on earth I would want there. Richard was ready to hire extra security, should that be needed. However, the hospital staff had to hear this from the horse's mouth if they were to ban the woman who was still my legal spouse.

Richard's journal entry states that the nurses lowered my sedation level just enough so that, "Jackie the social worker was able to have him explain with thumbs up and down that he didn't want his wife here. Mission accomplished!" The hospital called my wife to tell her she was not welcome, and she called back to say that she was coming anyway. Richard expressed his concerns about this to Richard the security guard, and the ex-military man retorted, "She won't get by me!" According to Richard my pseudo-brother, "He looked willing and ready to back it up!" Having a security guard on my side was very reassuring.

And so the concerned parties fell more or less into a routine. Dr. Whatmore, the director of the ICU who checked in on me periodically, said at least once, "This is worse than a horror film, maybe the worst I've seen." Richard noted that Dr. Hinckley made similar comments.

Part of Richard's and Ron's routine the first couple of days was running interference with the press, who were prowling like wolves outside the hospital doors, smelling a hot story. In this part of the country, a grizzly mauling is big news and mine had several elements that made it especially spicy: I had been mauled before, I had studied grizzlies and had published two books about them, my survival was in question, and the Park Service had suggested that I was unlawfully photographing bears when I was attacked. So the hospital, Richard, and later Ron fed the press scraps of information and mostly ran interference. The last thing I needed now was to answer a bunch of questions from reporters who would probably embellish the story or get it wrong.

In my drug-induced coma, I had no idea what the press was doing with my story but when I came to, it became clear that giving them more information about my condition would only make things worse. The last thing I ever want to do is to fuel a fire of public opinion that would inevitably lead to more sensationalized, negative publicity about grizzlies. This was one of the typical stories that appeared after my mauling:

From the *Bozeman Daily Chronicle*:

The man mauled by a grizzly bear in Yellowstone National Park Wednesday was Jim Cole, a Bozeman photographer, author and musician, the National Park Service announced Thursday.

After seven hours of emergency surgery on his badly wounded face, Cole, 57, remained in intensive care Thursday, according to Rich Berman, a friend at his bedside at the hospital in Idaho Falls, Idaho.

Cole, well known in the Bozeman area for his advocacy for

protecting grizzly bears and their habitat, was unable to speak and was breathing through a ventilator and being fed through a tube, Berman said. Cole can understand questions and answer them with a thumbs up or thumbs down hand signal . . .

. . . Cole's surgeon told Berman that the wounds did not appear to be predatory because there were no bite marks on his head or chest. Berman said he believed his friend probably came too close to a protective mother bear.

Most grizzly attacks occur when someone surprises a bear or comes too close to one protecting cubs or a food source . . .

. . . He was *photographing* [emphasis mine] bears in the Hayden Valley's Trout Creek drainage, prime grizzly habitat, Wednesday when the encounter happened, the Park Service said. He was hiking alone, off trail, about two or three miles from the road when a female with a single cub attacked.

Notice the insinuation in the Park Service part of the story. According to them, I was photographing bears, something that was pure speculation and, in my opinion, lazy reporting. There was no evidence to suggest this; my camera had been impounded and the flash card could easily have been checked, and there was nothing in the official reports to suggest that I had ever told anyone I had taken any photographs of bears. I had not. But the subtle message was that I had been doing something illegal. In the coming days I would take heat from bloggers, some of whom suggested I deserved what happened.

Ron and Richard knew that if reporters got a look at my stomach-churning injuries, the sensationalism factor of the story would triple. "We didn't talk much to the media," Ron said. "You had received a number of cards, flowers, and balloons from the major networks. One woman did annoy us. I think she was a producer from ABC in Denver, and she was out there to make initial contacts. She came into the family waiting room, acting like she was there for a patient, while Richard and I were having a discussion with Dr. Hinckley. She was kind of lying in wait, waiting for Dr. Hinckley to leave. Then she approached and asked us if we were with the man who was attacked by the grizzly bear. We asked her to leave, but after that, she turned out to be pretty nice and professional."

Why the media blackout? When I do my lectures at schools, I always come across with the attitude that this is a beautiful animal, and that for the most part there is nothing to fear from them if you keep your distance and give them space. I never put the blame on the bear. I have studied lots of attacks and I know the details of why they happened. Based on my prior attack, I knew what the press up here would do: publish huge, front-page headlines, "Man Savaged by Grizzly Bear." I didn't want people to blame the bear, kill the bear, or stay out of the parks because of misplaced fears.

Being a trained attorney, Ron took the role of note taker. Richard had his computer and did a good job of trying to put together a journal of what happened since he had been there practically from the beginning. From Richard's journal:

Saturday morning, 9:00 A.M., May 26th, beginning to wean Jim off the respirator. He is breathing on his own for the first time since arriving on May 23rd. Reason out for three days—nurses had tried to lighten Jim's level of sedation but his blood pressure rises. I was just telling Pamela, one of Jim's nurses, that we've been together two straight days and haven't argued about politics, Limbaugh, or the importance of conservative values. She was impressed with the way Jim is responding.

I was finally breathing on my own and was now able to understand the human voice, although I couldn't yet speak. I responded to Richard and Ron by squeezing their hands. A couple of hours later, about 1 P.M., I slowly awoke and the decision was made to lower my medications even further to extubate me. I began to mutter. I was blind in both eyes but I'm not sure when this realization first hit me. When I finally was really conscious, Ron and Richard's voices were the first sounds I remember hearing. This was one of the most amazing moments of my life. What could have been more comforting than to rise up through the foggy maze with the two people closest to me in the world right there at my bedside? I may have been without technical eyesight but I could see these two characters perfectly. In the rich tradition of The Smothers Brothers, Abbott and Costello, Martin and Lewis, and Gleason and Carney, these guys put on quite a show.

While I was sitting up waiting to be extubated, Ron's back was turned when I held up two fingers. He heard the nurse say "two." Then I held up five fingers and he heard the nurse say "five." Ron instantly knew that I was gesturing the famous two-fifty pinochle bid. This indicated to him that I was okay, coherent, and still the joker. Ron said, "At this point, I knew you were back." Perhaps nothing else short of my getting up and walking out of the hospital at that moment could have eased my two friends' minds as much.

Richard asked, "Do you know where you are? Do you know why you're here?" Some seconds later, I shook my head no. "You're in Idaho. You were mauled by a bear." This was all meaningless to me. Richard thinks that the information didn't register because I couldn't correlate Idaho and being mauled.

He tried again. "You were mauled by a bear in Yellowstone. You were airlifted to this hospital in Idaho. Do you know what happened?" I again shook my head. The heavy painkillers helped me remain reasonably comfortable in my mangled state, but disoriented me profoundly. The one stabilizing factor was Richard's and Ron's comforting, familiar presence. From Richard's journal:

> May 26th, 1:30. Jim is talking up a storm, calling me a schlepper. Didn't remember anything about the attack so I didn't say much. Jim's sense of humor is intact. He and Ron keep laughing about two-fifty, two-fifty, two-fifty. I need to go to Target and get something to record the audio because it is unbelievable what Jim is saying and singing. Everyone is very relieved!

Right there in the EIRMC ICU, Ron and I treated the staff to an impromptu concert of "Harrigan," "Yankee Doodle Dandy," and "Over There," from our all-time favorite movie, *Yankee Doodle Dandy,* starring James Cagney as George M. Cohan.

I was in a kind of memory Twilight Zone with no recollection of the attack. But at about 5:00 that evening, during a low-key chit-chat with my two bosom buddies, the light bulb suddenly switched on. I blurted out, "I remember now," and remember I did. I proceeded to narrate the entire gruesome episode in all the vivid detail that my memory could muster.

Richard was at my bedside listening and prompting me with pertinent questions while Ron took thorough notes, writing as fast and legibly as possible while I rambled on. They later told me that the heavy medication I was on acted like truth serum; despite the Park Service account, there was no longer any doubt about what happened. When I said I was "ambushed" and related the part about the bear tunneling under my body, I was so animated that it appeared like I really thought the bear was doing this to me as I spoke. In my delirium, I said, "Please tell me that the bear is not around." As I dozed after my story, I was apparently moaning and saying, "Help me God!" Ron and Richard felt that I was recalling the mauling but I didn't remember any of those spontaneous exclamations when I awoke.

On Saturday, May 26th, my first conscious night since the mauling, I didn't sleep a wink. For the first time in my life, my entire being felt vulnerable and fragile, closer to the abyss than ever before. In this supremely drugged state, I made Richard promise that he wouldn't leave me. I felt petrified and extremely insecure. Richard spent the entire night in my room and got very little shuteye because I was totally wound up and never stopped chattering. From that night on, Ron and Richard alternated staying with me at night so that at least one of them was with me around the clock. Who could ask for more?

During that first night, an intense reliving of the attack scared the pants off of me. I started shivering. At one point I was vividly hallucinating, visibly and verbally reliving the encounter moment by moment, though I don't recall making any vocalizations during the actual attack. Richard later said that I really believed the bear was in the room; I was saying things like, "Oh my God! I feel it right now." I tried to cover my head but couldn't. Richard got up to reassure me by identifying himself, holding my hand, and saying "two-fifty" whenever he needed to. It worked. "Two-fifty" became my touchstone throughout my recovery.

I called out to Richard often during this first sleepless night to make sure he was there. Paul Thomas, a marvelous night-shift nurse, actually reprimanded me for being tough on Richard. "Let him get some sleep!" he told me more than once. I can still hear Paul's sincere, frustrated, but tactful scolding. But I simply couldn't stop talking. I remember sincerely promising that I would shut my yap but each time, these vows lasted only minutes or even seconds.

As I have said, the first time I was mauled by a grizzly in 1993, I never had a single dream about the incident. This time the mauling was far more severe. My first conscious night was one of intense, dramatic nightmares. But after that night, never again have I dreamt about the incident. Go figure.

The second night was Ron's shift. He boasted how he would be able to sleep through anything. Poor, droopy-eyed, battle-fatigued Richard just chuckled. I have seen "The Vulture" perfectly comfortable and snoring away in a simple metal chair with thin cushions, the type that I can barely sit on comfortably. Well, the sleeping master met his match this time. The decent-looking reclining chair next to the bed turned out to be terribly uncomfortable even by Ron's standards. Nurses were constantly in and out to check my vital signs and give medications. The intermittent beeping of the IV feeding machine alone would challenge any world-class sleeper. However, the real reason that Ron couldn't sleep was that same protective, paternal instinct my father had. At every utterance or alarm, he awoke to make sure that nothing was wrong. After ensuring himself that all was okay, he would try to catch a few more winks. It was very sweet and touching, though not great for Ron's state of mind.

That night, while Ron was sitting with me, the door opened. "I was sitting in Jim's room at 11:30 at night, Jim was sleeping, and I was reading," Ron told Tim later. "I saw a shadow, and one of my concerns was people trying to get in, especially reporters. I was about to stand up and challenge the person, but it was Dr. Hinckley with his son, checking on Jim. They had been to a sporting event and had swung by to make sure everything was okay. So we sat and chatted and he asked some questions about what we had observed with Jim. That impressed the hell out of me."

I asked Dr. Hinckley about this late-night call and he said, "There's a story about a farmhand who, every night before he went to bed, made sure that every door and window on the farm was closed tightly. The farmer always shook his head at this because the weather was warm and mild. But one night a fierce storm came rolling in, and the farmer ran out and woke the farmhand so they could batten down the hatches before the storm hit. The farmhand told the farmer to relax; he had already taken care of it, like he did every night. He did it so he could sleep soundly. That's what I do—stop in and make sure all the doors and windows are closed with my patients so I can sleep soundly."

My concept of time was completely distorted. Every day felt excruciatingly long. I would ask someone what time it was after what seemed like a long period only to find out that just a few minutes had passed. Some days, it felt like there was no end in sight. But this was far better than the alternative.

My pain threshold was also apparently in the Twilight Zone. Nurses forewarned me about the painful abdominal rabies shots they were about to administer and all I'd feel was a little tickle in my belly. I never felt pain during either of my two hikes for life. Both times my body was in a serious state of shock and loaded with adrenaline. Had I been in significant pain I couldn't have done anything about it, but I don't remember any pain, just fighting and methodically churning forward on those strong legs that my father had bequeathed to me.

It was an interesting few days. I was sleep-deprived and had a severe case of diarrhea of the mouth. My monologues simply would not cease; I was that wired. "Motor Mouth" became my nickname around the ICU. In the three days after I became conscious I think I got about three hours of sleep total; I simply never could relax my mind. There must have been a lot going on in my mutilated head that provoked intense, spontaneous outbursts. Hallucinations floated around me as my body processed gigantic doses of the pain medication that allowed me to maintain a reasonable comfort level. This was unnerving and left me feeling quite vulnerable. My prescription? Endless chatter, which allowed me to hear my own voice and experience my own memories and confirm that, yes, I was still here, I was alive.

During my constant monologues, I retold the same story over and over: my father's great bunker shot during the last round of golf of his life. Dutifully and patiently, the EIRMC staff listened again and again to my tale.

It was March of 1999, and my father, Robert Cole, and I were on the father–son road trip of a lifetime, cruising the gorgeous Pacific Coast Highway in California and enjoying the golf courses and atmosphere of the world-famous Pebble Beach area. We had already had a memorable trip when March 10th dawned, but we had an even more promising day ahead: our one round of golf for the trip, on the Inn and Links at Spanish Bay.

Spanish Bay was bright and blustery, and this made the course even more challenging than usual. We found out quickly that if you didn't hit the ball straight, it meant big trouble. Our play was erratic, but we had great fun although neither one of us made a single par on the front nine. At one poignant moment on the back nine, Dad commented to me what a special privilege it was for us to be sharing a day like this together. As always, we both tried our best but ultimately didn't really care about our score. How could we? This was a cruelly unforgiving target course designed by professionals for highly skilled players. We just relished the time together, scorecard or no scorecard.

This memory stands out so clearly for me: On the thirteenth hole, a short but tricky par three, Dad plugged his tee shot into the left bunker. It would have been easy to blast out of the sand only to end up in the bunker directly across the narrow green. To complicate matters, this trap was set up at a steep uphill angle that would test anyone's balance. My dad handled this shot like a pro. He assumed a comfortable ball-striking position then began to wiggle his strong legs deep into the sand to get a firm foundation. I could see the definition in his leg muscles. He delicately brought the club back, then hit through the shot with exceptional balance. The ball flopped down softly and nestled within three feet of the hole.

"Great shot, Dad," I said.

"Thank you," he said without looking at me, then raked the sand and walked to his ball as though he hit that kind of shot every day. Quite the cool customer. Unbeknownst to either of us at the time, this would be the last par of his life.

A little over an hour later, we had just completed the picturesque but treacherous par-four seventeenth hole which runs right along the Pacific. Dad hadn't yet marked our scorecard as we stood together on the par-five eighteenth tee ready to begin the final hole of a great day. He was holding a driver in his right hand and a ball and tee in the golf glove on his left hand. In a calm voice, he said faintly, "I feel dizzy," and collapsed into my arms. He had a massive heart attack and never again saw the light of day.

My father died four days shy of his seventy-eighth birthday, two days after Joe DiMaggio, with his son at his side, doing what he loved and enjoying his life to the very last moment. His weight was too much for his twice-bypassed heart to handle, but his legs stayed strong to the end.

Ironically, a couple of weeks after I left EIRMC, Richard was playing golf in Boulder and found himself in a similar sand trap dilemma. He remembered the story, dug his feet into the sand in a similar fashion, and hit a great shot just like Dad did. One of his playing partners asked, "Have you been taking lessons?" Richard just grinned.

During my time in EIRMC, I was surrounded by some of the most incredible human beings I have ever known, starting with Richard and Ron. As the days went on the lack of sleep, stress, and questionable food took their toll. Richard soon caught a cold and was given a prescription by Dr. Hinckley. Ron was fighting sickness and losing his voice, and this bug ballooned into pneumonia when he returned home to Antioch, Illinois. They never complained.

Physical therapists like Kim Wilkes (who has since become a friend) came by daily to take me for walks through the EIRMC hallway system. My legs remained strong and I was able to walk very well with reasonable endurance even in my condition. It was in great part due to the efforts of professionals like Kim that I was able to trek back to the Hayden Valley site where I was attacked just a little over three months later.

Richard later told me that, during his middle of the night drive from Salt Lake City to Idaho Falls while I was still in surgery, he was extremely concerned and skeptical that a "small town" like Idaho Falls might not have adequate care. In his own words: "What kind of care and surgical staff are you going to get out here in the middle of Timbuktu?" Fortunately for me, they have some amazing folks in Timbuktu.

Richard watched the phenomenal care I was getting from the moment he arrived, then all night long. By the next morning, he was profoundly relieved to see that this hospital staff, from top to bottom, was very impressive. "Seeing is believing," he said. "I'm so glad that I was wrong. Little did I know that they are a very highly rated and respected trauma center."

EIRMC has a contract with Yellowstone Park to handle medical emergencies, including animal attacks. As I stated earlier, bear maulings are extremely rare in the park, but previous victims who came to EIRMC have left in one piece. A plethora of awards for excellence decorate a wing of the hallway near the main lobby. EIRMC is owned by Health Corporation of America, giving it a strong financial base. The hospital benefits tremendously from top-notch recruiting and exceptional neurosurgeons.

The EIRMC ICU staff was really unbelievable. The nurses,

who had to listen to me yammer day and night, were attentive, kind, and reassuring. Doctors came by my room several times a day. This exceptional hospital staff was supportive to me in every way imaginable. They put up a big yellow sign on my hospital room door that read in bold black lettering, NO VISITORS. INQUIRE AT DESK. Only room 217 bore this warning. It occurred to me later that they fiercely protected me like the mother bear whose defense of her cub put me in this predicament in the first place.

I inquired about the availability of a guitar and sent Ron on a mission. Lo and behold, they located one within the hospital's rehabilitation unit. They loaned it to me on one condition: I had to autograph it for them. I would learn the whole story months later. In my weakened and hazy state, it was extremely difficult to play, not to mention that I was blind. I requested a capo and tuner for the guitar but did not expect that someone would go out and buy them. Nancy Brown, EIRMC Community Relations Specialist, went out and personally purchased a capo and pitch pipe for me. She later confided that had this guitar not been available, she would have loaned me hers.

Thanks to her, I managed to pick and sing a few tunes, although the old instrument buzzed when I couldn't hold the strings down cleanly with my left hand. At the time I thought it was a bad guitar, but I didn't consider that my left hand was weakened, having been bitten by the mother bear. Unbeknownst to me, my playing and singing drew a crowd that gathered around my hospital room door. Merle and Doc Watson would have been proud. Though I never played that guitar again, it was comforting knowing it was in the room, just in case. Because I was still so weak, my guitar picking was suspended until I was reunited with the Martin guitar that I purchased in Chicago way back in the summer of 1971.

Nancy Brown also held the paparazzi at bay. Some members of the press corps did manage to slip in under the radar to eavesdrop on private conversations, so upon Richard's request, my close friend Michael Sanders assumed the burden of dealing with all media inquiries until I was able to take over many months later.

Paul Thomas (nicknamed "Tall Paul") was assigned to me for my pivotal first two conscious nights in the hospital for good reason. He was strong and forceful, easily able to put me in my place when necessary. I'm a fiercely independent person and often very stubborn. He was stern and direct with a wry sense of humor. From him, I received the tough love that I needed at that time. He was the bad guy who often took Ron and Richard off the hook. As the days passed by, Paul and I came to understand each other perfectly.

Richard later recounted the story of a nurse who really touched our lives, though I have no recollection of these events. She first saw me in the emergency room on the afternoon of May 23rd, prior to my nine-hour surgery. She told Richard that she had heard my story from the hospital staff and dreamed about me that night. She couldn't get my plight out of her mind and just had to come in the next day to check on my

A black bear runs directly across the trail closely behind two unsuspecting hikers.

At the foot of picturesque
Grinnell Lake in the Glacier
Park backcountry.

This big bear carefully enters the river and lays claim to a prime fishing spot recently vacated by a much larger male.

In a rare sighting, a powerful male grizzly drags an elk carcass through the snow on Christmas Eve in Yellowstone, 2008.

The always vigilant mama bear, who I knew as a cub, constantly surveys the scene as she calmly nurses her triplets.

These two subadult siblings playfully growl and bare their teeth, nose to nose.

This quilled bear hopefully learned an important survival lesson: slow moving porcupines aren't as benign as they look.

The young bruin stands on a sandbar, chewing and crunching a waterlogged stick.

The cautious big male stands like a man for a better look at his domain along an open ridge in Yellowstone country.

A tiny cub scurries to keep pace with mom during the early spring in Yellowstone.

Bears often share the trails as I yell over this one's head to warn oncoming hikers on the Iceberg Lake Trail in Glacier Park.

This wide-eyed sniffing mother bear checks out Yellowstone traffic as two spring cubs follow her lead.

As mom fishes nearby, her three wary cubs take on human-like postures to get a better look at the activities of other bears in the river.

After scampering up to safety, these two anxious cubs impatiently wait for mom to call them down.

With my father on the golf course. About an hour after this picture was taken, my father had a massive heart attack and collapsed in my arms on the 18th tee.

This is likely the mother bear who tore my face off as I observed her in a nonthreatening situation just over one year after the attack in Yellowstone.

The sharp switchbacks of Trout Creek in Hayden Valley were a great privilege to witness from a vastly different perspective one year later.

condition. "She was very caring, very impressed with your ability to fight. She called you a 'survivor,'" Richard said to me.

A couple of days later when I was off the respirator, she entered room 217 in her official capacity as a pulmonary nurse. To perform the pulmonary function test, my job was to blow into a tube filled with small light balls. According to Richard, "The balls just stayed up there forever. The nurse was blown away. She said you had the lung capacity of a twenty- to thirty-year-old."

On one of their walks to the motel room that Richard had rented, Richard and Ron talked about the unbelievable care, personal attention, and empathy I had received at EIRMC. "Jim would not have gotten anything like the care and concern that he did from a hospital in any major metropolitan area," Ron said to Tim. "To this day, it amazes me. One of his nurses was an attractive blonde who was putting a catheter in, and we told her later that it was a good thing Jim couldn't see her because she would have had a much harder time putting the catheter in. She just smiled and laughed as we joked, and another time, she said to me and Richard, 'I'm going to recommend you guys for a psych consult.' That's when we knew Jim was going to be all right, when people were able to joke about things like that." The citizens of this region are fortunate to have access to a facility of this caliber.

My overall condition was steadily improving as my weakened body gained physical and emotional strength with each passing day. My second surgery occurred about a week after I entered the hospital. This relatively minor procedure consisted primarily of cleaning up loose ends and removing packing from my nose. Finally, after nine days in the intensive care unit I transferred to a regular hospital room on the fifth floor. I had spent all those days spaced out on a drug called Fentanyl (a hundred times more potent than morphine), which had me thinking that I was in a different room each night. Richard broke the rules and unhooked me a few minutes early without permission of the nurse, because I just couldn't wait to be out of there. Before leaving, I asked Richard, "Have I been in the same room every night?" and he shocked me when he answered, "Yes."

Upon arrival at my new regular medical unit on the fifth floor Thursday afternoon, I was feeling my oats and eagerly wanted to become acclimated to my new surroundings. Richard remembered, "You said, 'I've seen Doc Watson do this a hundred times.' You thought you could go in the room and immediately become familiar with it by touching everything. You were out of control and wouldn't listen to anything I had to say until your hands accidentally slipped into the toilet bowl." Okay, orienting myself to the new room was far more difficult than I expected. I never did figure out where everything was.

Richard became more frustrated because I wouldn't sit still in bed. He was afraid I would injure myself, so he called a nurse. The nurse asked me to stay in bed then went on to explain to Richard that the bed was equipped with an alarm that senses when a patient gets out of bed. They decided to activate it. It was like being in a fire station during a natural disaster.

"As I started to walk down the hall," Richard said, "I wasn't ten feet out of the room when the alarm was blaring. You couldn't sit still in bed for thirty seconds."

The nurse came back in and reiterated the importance of staying in bed. She made it clear that I could call a nurse at any time with the remote device on the bed next to my right hand. This knocked some sense back to me. After that I was a (relatively) good boy. Nurses checked in throughout the following day. Kim Wilkes dropped by to take me for a tour through the hallways. But it was a challenging and disorienting day because I was being weaned from the constant support of my two surrogate brothers. Richard and Ron had driven four hours back to Yellowstone to try and retrieve some of my possessions from my van, which was still being held by the Park Service. I spent the majority of the afternoon listening to a Chicago Cubs baseball game on television.

Late in the evening Richard and Ron returned. Ron had called the Park Service but had gotten the runaround. The rangers said they couldn't release the items without the U.S. Attorney's approval. The attorney assigned to Yellowstone was unavailable, so Ron called the U.S. Attorney's office in Cheyenne, Wyoming, to explain the urgent need for the items. After ducking Park Service red tape they were able to secure my wallet, medications, address book, appointment book, guitar, shoes, and some clothes. Park Service personnel refused to release my van, camera equipment, computer, or cell phone (they told Ron I "might have used it to take photos of a bear," something that's not illegal as long as you don't intentionally approach a bear within hundred yards), but at least I was now back in possession of some essential items.

On Saturday, I couldn't take it anymore. I was bored and craved fresh air. "He wanted to go visit the ER to meet a few of the people," Ron said to Tim later. "We got him a floppy fisherman's hat and some Roy Orbison sunglasses. He was quite a sight. We went down to the ER, and Jim met some of the staff and did a little jig for them. They said they don't get return visits very often from the people who come through the ER. There are points of the whole experience that you just have to look back on and laugh." I thanked one and all for their efforts and told everyone what a great staff they were. I also told them that I would be back, and that was a promise I intended to keep.

I was clearly ready to leave EIRMC, but just as clearly I needed additional treatment. The $64,000 question was, where did I go from Idaho? Heading home to Montana was not a viable option. I needed more surgery and wanted the best surgeons. Richard was speaking constantly with my close friend Molly Kiser (the nurse who had helped me recover from my first mauling) about my options. As I found out later, she was hard at work behind the scenes. Through her various contacts she arranged for my admission to the University of Colorado hospital in Denver. Total self-sufficiency would not be an option when I left University Hospital, so it was decided that I would stay with Richard and his wife Elle for a while after that and Molly would oversee my recovery. I remain humbled that these wonderful people were doing all this on my behalf.

The second question was, how would I get there? I had no desire to deal with airport security and I doubted I could fly with anything resembling comfort on a cramped commercial airliner. Auto travel would have taken at least twelve hours. Richard made all these concerns moot: he chartered a private plane. As the late, great Cubs announcer Harry Caray would have said, "Holy cow!"

Meanwhile, Richard's son Bret had sent a fabulous gift: a classic, vintage remastered collection of Louis Armstrong tunes. On my last night in Idaho, Richard popped them into his computer one at a time and I was blown away. This was the first music I had heard since my arrival in Idaho Falls and the great Louis Armstrong has always been one of my all-time favorites.

In the summer of 1958 or 1959, I came home sweaty and covered with dirt from a pony league baseball game. Louis Armstrong was scheduled to perform a sold-out show at Ravinia Park, just three blocks from our house, and I wanted to go. My mother said, "Let's give it a try." I hurriedly showered, put on presentable clothes and was out the door. Mom yelled out, "Good luck!"

At Ravinia I scoped around for someone with an extra ticket. An elderly lady was looking around and never one to be shy, I asked her if she had an extra ticket. Amazingly, she said yes. She explained that her husband was sick and unable to attend and that I was welcome to join her. It seemed like she was looking for someone whom she would be comfortable sitting with and a well-groomed friendly child was obviously to her liking. I paid her face value and we strolled in together.

Well, it turned out that this nice lady was a season ticket holder with some of the best seats in the house, sixth row just to the viewer's right of center stage! I remember like it was yesterday: a command performance by an aging legend, replete with his greatest hits accompanied by a full ensemble of backup musicians. I can still see Satchmo's classic mannerisms, including his trademark wiping of sweat off his shiny black forehead between songs with a white handkerchief in his left hand. This was an indelible moment in time, and this music brought that joy back to me in the hospital. What a gift.

It has always been harder to say good-bye to Ron than any other person who has crossed my life. The very early morning of June 3, 2007, was no exception. He abruptly awoke with his cell phone alarm, we hugged, and he was out the door. He had to get to the airport to catch a flight to Chicago through Seattle. He's the "Funny Man" of the song that's excerpted at the start of this chapter, and I was sorry to lose the ebullient sense of humor that had seen me through some dark days. I wept when he left.

A few hours later, Richard came into the room. Time to pack up and get ready to roll. This was easier said than done. Richard rarely packs for himself; he has flown out to visit me in Montana more than once with literally just the clothes on his back. Now he had to pack for us both. Finally, we headed down to the lobby.

When I left EIRMC, it was Sunday morning, June 3rd. I had been there for eleven days. I vowed to return. I knew that when my vision was restored and I was back on my feet, my emotions would compel me to match faces to voices and express a heartfelt thank you to everyone who helped me—face to face, my one eye to their two. To Richard's amazement, a stretch limousine pulled up to the hospital at the appointed time. Richard had expected a jeep, but I guess this is one of the perks you get when you fly like a jet-setter. The driver, who would also be our pilot, placed our luggage in the trunk and pulled away from the Eastern Idaho Regional Medical Center entrance toward the highway. Next stop: Colorado, the home of my old life and my unimaginable near-future.

7

Coming Back to Life

Indians went to grizzly school to learn about their food
They watched the bears eat plants used for medicines
As mighty spirit guardians, grizzlies were the teachers
Master gatherers and spirit healers
Kindred spirits, nitakyaio, kindred spirits, nitakyaio

—"Kindred Spirits," music and lyrics by James R. Cole

IT WAS A LUXURIOUS ride to the airport and an equally luxurious flight that Richard enjoyed with childlike enthusiasm while I never saw a thing. I doubt that either of us would ever spring for such an extravagance again, but it seamlessly returned me to the civilized world for an evening. Richard's wonderful wife, Elle, met us at the airport, drove us home, and cooked a spectacular dinner. The evening was a breath of fresh air for me. Though I was nervous about being on my own without a nurse for even one night, it felt great to be back out in the world again and there's nothing like home cooking.

On my only night away from a hospital during this three-week stretch, Richard and Elle checked in on me throughout the night. I slept soundly and never heard so much as a peep from them.

The next day, it was back to hospital life. Richard drove me to Denver and I checked into University Hospital, where it was comforting to receive a private room. Settling in, I had no idea that the entire hospital was moving to a brand new facility within two weeks. The downside: the kitchen was being dismantled so the food was marginal at best.

That was remedied the following evening when Richard and Elle came down from Boulder to check up on me. They brought good food and most importantly my guitar, which was invaluable in helping me get through the long, lonely days and nights. Sometimes when I was having trouble sleeping, I would get up and quietly pick some tunes until I felt tired.

Exploratory surgery came Wednesday so the doctors could figure out what they were dealing with. They removed a great deal of Jello-like mush—consisting of liquefied dead tissue— that was embedded in my face, while evaluating my general condition. When the nurses rolled me into the recovery room, I almost instantly popped up out of bed and asked, "Am I supposed to feel this good?" The nurses were blown away. One of them said, "Nobody ever has!"

By this time, with the exception of breakfast, I was asking the hospital staff not to bring me any meals. When a gentleman server asked me why, I retorted, "I'm in here to get better." He laughed.

Molly came down that evening with grocery supplies. Always the concerned and vigilant caretaker, she brought me grapes, turkey, provolone cheese, and matzo ball soup, all of which took up half of the space in the refrigerator at the nurses' station. Slipping into nurse mode, Molly also quickly made friends with the staff, asking every question that she deemed important and following up until she got satisfactory answers. She earned the respect of the entire staff. If she was unable to attend an important doctor visit, she participated over the phone and didn't miss a beat. She was a marvelous advocate, something that is proved to enhance patient outcomes.

The doctor came in the morning after the surgery and lifted my right eyelid. My vision wasn't 100 percent, but I could see and this was positively sensational. The lid was still not functioning properly but I could lift it up with my hand anytime I really wanted to see something. This was a major step in regaining my independence. Just navigating around the room to grab my guitar or visit the bathroom was much easier with one eye open.

Molly came to visit most days, bringing fresh supplies and taking my order from Whole Foods. She also began to take me for long walks outside the hospital; it was a precious gift to be outside in the fresh air again, even if it was in the city.

Strong pain medication administered every two hours helped me to sustain a reasonable level of comfort. Molly was in the room when a nurse first offered morphine. Addiction was my first thought and I balked at the idea. But both Molly and the nurse were adamant that it would not be a problem given the doses I would get. So I said, "Why not? Live it up!" The morphine provided almost instant relief and a pleasant feeling with each dose. It became very apparent to me how people could get addicted to this drug, but I could never conceive of sticking a needle in my arm like that.

My next surgery was scheduled for Tuesday, June 10th. The night before, I had a somber phone discussion with Richard. He was reluctant to say what everybody else already knew: although I had amazingly dodged any serious infection of my wounds, it would take a miracle for me to ever have use of my left eye again. Breaking the bad news was harder for him than it was for me. I knew which side of my face the bear had raked with her claws, and it didn't take a physician to surmise that my left eye had taken a beating. Hearing the news shook me up, but I also knew I was lucky to be alive and that the long-term prognosis for my right eye was now good.

Bottom line, I wanted to know my health status, good or bad. I thanked him and, as had become my nightly routine, spent the remainder of the evening winding down with mellow guitar tunes while listening to David Letterman in the background.

There was no bone structure left in my face after the bear tore it off. Dr. Hinckley at EIRMC had used a mesh of titanium to support my new artificial face. My surgeons, Dr. John Campana and Dr. Vikram Durairij, were concerned that the titanium might be causing or encouraging infection so they replaced it with silicone. They were also concerned that the mesh near my left eye was embedded too far, thus preventing the eyelid from functioning. They repaired this as well.

I was later told that in order to have a fully functioning left eye, two things needed to happen. First, the eyelid had to function properly. Second, the left eyeball needed to have full range of motion to move in concert with the right eye. If it didn't, but the lid was moving properly, I'd experience double vision and would be required by common sense to keep my left eye covered. Given the extent of the damage, the chance of one of these functional movements coming back at full strength was extremely remote. I was learning more than I ever wanted to know about the medical world.

According to Dr. Durairij, "It would take a miracle" for both functions to return to normal. I had now heard the word "miracle" several times during my recovery. Physicians don't use the word very often. When they do, it's usually code for "There's nothing else that medicine can do." But I have some experience with miracles; I think my hike to safety was a miracle in itself. So though I could ultimately accept this verdict, I wasn't about to give up.

Following this surgery I was full of energy and ready to roll. My right eyelid was beginning to function on its own. Now at least I had limited vision without manual assistance. Then things got better: on Wednesday the doctors said that my discharge that very day was a distinct possibility. After lying in drug-induced repose in hospital beds for three straight weeks, I was dying to get out. In addition, the hospital was moving to the new location and wanted everybody out who was able. I was happy to oblige.

After a thorough evaluation and discussion with Molly and me about wound care, pain medication, handling emergencies, and not overexerting myself (did they know me or what?), the staff announced that I was ready, willing, and able to go. I sat down in the required wheelchair and someone finally wheeled me through the long white-tiled hallway, down the elevator for the last time, then out the door. Molly walked me to her car in a steady rain. The cool droplets soaking into my hair and T-shirt reminded me that it was great to be alive. I was ready to throw myself on the mercy of Richard and Elle's hospitality.

Molly drove me up Interstate 25 toward Boulder, got me to Richard and Elle's house, and helped me get my things set up in the palatial basement suite. I had a king-size Tempurpedic mattress, a west-facing window with a view of a concrete window well and my own bathroom. Elle is a former restaurateur and she prepared the first of many incredible meals for me that evening. It was quite an upgrade from hospital quarters and mystery food.

I needed the food. I was down to 148 pounds on my five-foot-nine-inch frame. I've always been lean due to all the exercise I get hiking in the backcountry, but it had been decades since I actually needed to put on weight. Now I was back to a weight I hadn't seen since I was a teenager. I was happy to indulge myself with the wonderful food my hosts provided.

As the days went along, it also became clear that I essentially had my own personal nursing staff. Molly had assumed the role of my personal nurse and came over at least once a day to change the dressing on the gaping hole in my left cheek. When she had to deal with the affairs of her own life, including working twelve-hour shifts at a local hospital, Laurel Beth Eisenschiml—a former nurse and close friend all the way back to kindergarten days at Braeside School in Highland Park, Illinois—pinch hit. In second grade, Laurel was my very first girlfriend; I recall many attempts to sneak peeks at her underpants. We have been close for a long time and I cherish her friendship.

One thing became clear to me as we settled into a routine: my security blanket was gone. I was no longer in the hospital with doctors and emergency facilities just steps away. This made my always-racing mind jump to a series of anxious "what if" questions. What if I developed an infection? What if I fell? I was feeling tentative and insecure in the early going and at one frustrating point, Richard and I questioned whether they had let me out of the hospital too soon. But there was no choice in the matter. My overall frame of mind was better away from the hospital and I needed to be doing things for myself as soon as possible.

For example, I had to put ointment in my eyes. At the hospital, nurses had done this. Now I had to do it without assistance, which was intimidating. I was afraid of causing further damage to my one good eye with the needle-nosed dispenser end of the small tube. But Molly showed me how to accomplish this task by releasing the ointment onto a Q-tip that was attached to the end of a long wooden stick. I could handle a Q-tip. If it inadvertently touched my eyeball, no big deal. Voilà! My dexterity improved daily.

But Molly must have noticed how tentative I was about being completely independent again. One day she sat me down for a tactful lecture on my need to wean myself from dependency on others (with the exception of the daily repacking of my face, which I could not do). I appreciated her gentle kick to the backside and took it to heart. It was time to get past my fear and apprehension and take the bull by the horns. If I was going to get back to full strength and get back into the wild doing what I loved, I would have to make it happen. So I set about it.

Boulder is surrounded by a greenbelt crisscrossed with more than 120 miles of trails, and the altitude gives any hiker a spectacular workout. At first, I was in no shape to get back into any sort of hiking routine, but I knew that setting that as my goal would motivate me to follow doctor's orders, let my body rest, get a lot of good food into my belly, and do all the things that would enable me to get my boots dirty in the near future.

Every day brought new challenges, but the most difficult obstacle was getting out of bed each morning. Part of me did not want to face the day; I knew I faced a long road. Some mornings during the first two weeks, I slept as late as 11 A.M., which is unheard of for me. I'm a morning person. But my body must have really needed the rest so I went with the flow.

I wasn't trail-ready, but I craved exercise. Within the first few days, riding the stationary bicycle in Richard's office became my favorite activity. The summer was hot and dry, so I stayed indoors in the heat of the day, mostly playing guitar. In fact, I practiced four to five hours a day for over a month. It was the most daily guitar time I've put in since the 1970s (though I don't recommend a bear mauling as a way to impose discipline). Because I was effectively blind, my friend Doc Watson, who has been blind his whole life, gave me clear instructions over the phone on how to put new strings on my guitar without eyesight. I then painstakingly pieced together the groundwork for a new song, "Blindsided," as one way of recounting the bear attack. In addition, after an inspirational discussion with Richard that planted the seed, Elle set me up with a computer on an old dining room table and I began writing this book.

After a couple of weeks, Molly began taking me for beautiful hikes on the Boulder trail system and the occasional longer outings to Caribou Ranch Open Space and Rocky Mountain National Park. At this point I preferred flat trails even if the scenery was compromised. My stamina had suffered from the forced inactivity and I simply couldn't easily handle elevation gain—yet. Molly and Richard also took me on the one-mile loop hike behind Richard's house. There, in the shade of the trees, I spotted turtles, fish, and a great blue heron fishing in one of the oval ponds circled by the trail. It was nice to see wildlife again, even if it was in tamer circumstances than usual. As my right eye improved, I was able to solo on this unchallenging hike. Another step forward.

I am not a warm weather person. I prefer the brisk chill of early morning, which dovetails nicely with my tendency to be up with the roosters. So I started rising early to get my miles in before the day heated up. My routine started out conservatively with only about three miles a day. But over the weeks, the daily distance gradually increased to about eight miles. Hiking was almost always the first thing I did in the morning. I leveled off at eight miles per morning for the final six weeks in Boulder—not a long hike for me, but certainly an achievement in my physical state.

As my energy grew, time began to roll along faster. The days, which had seemed interminable in the hospital, started to fly. Order was slowly returning to my life. The Boulder summer passed as I attended diligently to medical needs, exercised daily, practiced the guitar, and caught Cubs and White Sox games and other sporting events on television (baseball fans will remember that was the year of the Colorado Rockies' improbable run to the World Series). My social calendar was about as full as I wanted it to be as many gracious friends picked me up, wined and dined me at restaurants and in their homes, and dropped me back home. I felt privileged to be part of the civilized world again.

I owe Richard and Elle endless thanks for opening their home to me and putting up with me during those many weeks. It can't have been easy, especially since they had only been married for just over a year when I invaded. I don't know what Elle's wedding wishes were, but I doubt, "Have my home taken over by a scruffy, one-eyed naturalist with a hiking fetish and a baseball addiction" was on the list.

Richard, bless him, is honest about my stay in the way that only great friends can be. "In some ways he was a big pain in the ass, but in other ways he was a perfect patient," he says to Tim. "Everything to the letter the docs asked him to do, he did. He started doing acupuncture to regenerate his facial nerves and at one point had needles sticking out of his face. There was a tremendous risk of infection behind his cheeks and eyes, and the area had to be packed regularly and antibiotics put in. Molly would come to change his dressings and do what she needed to do. During all that, he was a perfect patient.

"Otherwise, he sometimes was a pain," my pal sarcastically continues. "In the early going when he was still heavily medicated, he would walk around the house in his underwear, and that didn't go over well. Later on, he went to a restaurant with Molly and because he was still partly blind and had a numb nose, he got a straw got stuck up his nose without feeling it, bled, and grossed out the whole restaurant, but he wouldn't leave. He said, 'I paid for this meal and I'm going to finish it.' That fierce independence came out, and that's why he's alive. As soon as he could walk, he tried to get in shape. He was driven, absolutely driven."

I plead guilty as charged, your honor. I was lucky enough to have incredibly understanding, empathetic caretakers. Richard came home every day for the first week I was there to bring or make lunch, but mostly to check up on me. When

Richard and Elle went out to dinner, which was frequently because they really enjoy dining out together (and it gave them some privacy), they often brought back a decadent chocolate dessert in a doggie bag to help put some meat back on my ribs. I'm an admitted food fanatic. I rarely eat desserts, but this was fun and Richard got a kick out of indulging me in this simple enjoyment. My ravenous urges are a daily struggle. If I didn't exercise so much and maintain discipline, I could easily have a weight problem.

One night early on, Richard came down and took a long look at my mug. Then he just shook his head and said softly, "You really got messed up." He told me that it was impossible for him to begin to imagine what I was going through and how difficult this all must be, especially for someone so fiercely independent. "I'm sure you had moments of incredible despair, but you never showed it. The first day you were here, you counted the fourteen steps so you could walk down to the basement without help and figured out where the light switch was. There was never any 'Why me?' and no f-bombs. Nothing. Because of that, I have even more respect for you than I had previously." That's my pal.

During the summer I revisited my surgeons, John Campana and Vikram Durairij, twice each at their offices south of Denver. Dr. Campana noted that my face had healed well, but a long complicated process of care lay ahead. His assessment was that I might need ten to twelve operations in the next couple of years (I've already had one since then) and would never look or function normally again. It would take ten to twelve months for my wounds to mature before additional surgery could be done. Dr. Campana suggested I maintain a beard for camouflage. He concluded in one of his patient summaries that this was an "atypical and complicated case. When I deal with an injury like this, I'm just glad the patient survived the assault."

My entire nose and most of my face were still numb. Dr. Campana told me that the nerves might regenerate at the pace of a millimeter per day, while Dr. Durairij bluntly stated that the nerves might never regenerate. Both doctors agreed that it was best for me not to have another surgery until summer 2008 at the soonest.

Thanks to Molly's investigative skills, I got busy seeking out alternative medical options. Dr. Rebecca Hutchins, a Behavioral Optometrist, was very helpful. She suggested hot and cold compresses on my eyes and face to help reduce the swelling and increase my comfort level. My left eye was still ballooned to almost Ping-Pong ball size. These simple compresses of only a washcloth and water produced a dramatic improvement within just a couple of days. This seemed to make a world of difference as the swelling noticeably began to subside.

When Dr. Hutchins suggested acupuncture, I felt foolish for not having thought of this myself. My past successes with acupuncture somehow never came to mind. Dr. Yun-Tao Ma's office, nicely finished in the basement of his house, was conveniently located just a short distance from Richard's home. Once a week for a month, Dr. Ma gave me extensive acupuncture treatments for my face and shoulder. He is a patient and understanding man although his soft-spoken, broken English sometimes makes him a challenge to comprehend.

Prior to the first appointment I told Dr. Ma's wife, who doubles as office manager, that I was soon headed back to Montana and my time with him would be limited. He said this would be a long process, then said he would to teach me how to do acupuncture on myself. I couldn't believe what I was hearing and immediately felt intimidated by this prospect. But he was dead serious and my mind had to be open to anything reasonable that would aid my recovery. So now each appointment included a self-acupuncture lesson. I was a human pincushion as I meticulously sank fifteen needles into my body every day—twelve in my face and three longer ones into my shoulder to treat the rotator cuff injury resulting from the impact of the collision with the mother bear. Both of my surgeons suggested that acupuncture was not likely to help because of the severe damage (the nerves were essentially gone on the left side) but they concurred that it couldn't hurt.

August came. It was time for me to return to my home in Bozeman. My doctors were encouraged by my recovery and my ability to care for myself. But before I left, Lynn Berman, Richard's ex-wife, and Molly took me to see Gordon Lightfoot at the historic Chautauqua Auditorium. I had witnessed many memorable performances at this venue over the years: Nancy Griffith, Tony Rice, Riders in the Sky, Norman Blake, and the great Steve Goodman from Chicago. A lot of memories lay behind those old walls.

Coming home was bittersweet. It was close to 11 P.M. on August 28th when my wife unlocked the door to my house just as I was reaching forward with the key, then went back to bed without a word as Richard and I entered. Seeing my dog, Merle, was extremely emotional, a joy beyond belief, as he soaked my face with warm happy licks. I really missed my little hound more than I could ever put into words.

I'd been away for a long time. A person just doesn't appreciate the little things until they are gone. Boy, did it feel good to sleep in my own bed. Ah, the simple pleasures of having access to my own belongings for the first time in a while. Friday was "Stock up the house day." Since presumably I would be stuck at home without the ability to drive for some time, Richard, Merle, and I spent the next day zigzagging around town executing remedial errands (grocery stores, post office, bank, insurance company, pharmacy, etc.) that would hopefully tide me over for a while.

I was glad to be back home, but at the same time, I was restless. I had been contemplating and anticipating a return to Hayden Valley for a long time, perhaps since a few days after regaining a semblance of awareness. The fact was, I wanted to get back into the field. To me, the true tragedy of this ordeal would not be the loss of sight in my left eye, but a lingering fear or doubt that kept me from doing what I loved: being a voice for the grizzly bear. I remember nurses in the Denver hospital asking me if I intended to go back into the wild, and each time I emphatically replied, "Yes."

Initially, I had not included Richard in my plans because I

did not think he would be comfortable in that type of back-country situation. He was also out of shape for a round-trip hike of at least eight miles with no trails. I was relatively strong, though far from mid-season form. Because of my perception of the limits of my eyesight, I wasn't ready to venture back into the Yellowstone wilderness alone. But I was eager to get out there and remember other wondrous things I had seen in Hayden Valley.

One time, I was enjoying three late autumn days in Yellowstone that had been some of the most glorious I'd ever seen in my life, with crisp, cold nights. I was hiking in Hayden Valley during the early morning when I heard the unmistakable sound of wolves howling in the distance. I hiked about half a mile to the top of a knoll to see if I could spot them. With my binoculars, I spied two wolves heading away from Trout Creek to the north. I figured that they must have a kill down there. Then I saw more wolves, black and gray, following the first pair. By the time I finished counting, there were fifteen wolves briskly walking in single file away from the creek to the north and disappearing over the hill.

Just after that, I spotted a large grizzly emerging from the forest to the south. The bear headed downhill rapidly toward the very spot the wolves had just vacated, sniffing around for ten minutes but not consuming anything from what I could see. Then he sniffed the air to the north and began to follow the same route as the wolf pack: over the big hillside to the north and out of sight. It was clear that he was trailing the pack and would attempt to pilfer some of their kills, though fifteen big wolves surrounding a carcass would be a formidable challenge for any grizzly.

I broached the subject of hiking back to the attack site to Richard, expecting to be barked at. But he surprised me with his interest, although he was not jumping for joy. He knew how eager I was to return to the scene. We agreed that the next day, we would forge our way to the attack site. Richard unselfishly tries to support his loved ones in every way. He turned out to be the perfect person with whom I could share this emotional experience.

On September 1, 2007, just three months and one week after the attack, we drove south toward Yellowstone. I was nervous, not surprisingly, but confident, as Richard's safety was now part of the equation. The weather was welcoming: partly cloudy and relatively cool after a blazing, record-breaking hot summer. Coming off another drought year, I really didn't expect to see much grizzly bear activity in Hayden Valley, especially in the middle of the day. It was a good year for white bark pine nuts, so I expected most grizzlies to be up high, not down in this valley. However, I promised a wary Richard that we would make plenty of noise and carry our cans of bear spray out of the holsters throughout the hike. My mauling had made him more fearful than ever of the great bear.

Richard parked the car on the east side of the Grand Loop Road and we headed directly uphill into the vast western portion of Hayden Valley. I led the charge and we must have sounded like a team of Rocky Balboa impersonators, yelling "Yo!, Yo!!, Yo!!!, Yo!!!!" with almost every step. This wasn't exactly my style, but I felt absolutely fantastic. It was a landmark day.

Later, Richard told me he was thinking, "I need a five to ten mile hike like a hole in the head." It's safe to say he would have preferred not to go. Early on, he became fearful and thought, "What the hell am I doing out here in grizzly territory?" His answer was simple. "After all you've been through, it's the least a 'brother' can do!" Our constant yelling made him feel more comfortable than the bear spray.

When we passed through familiar sandy thermal flats, I was astonished that the area was void of any remotely fresh grizzly bear sign of any kind. We observed very old diggings that were fairly fresh the last time I came through these parts three months ago, another lifetime. It was great to smell the outdoors again, though I was a bit tentative due to my altered vision. But I was effortlessly hiking at a strong pace and regaining confidence with every step. Richard later wrote in his journal, "After hiking for a few minutes, Jim became alive— the old Jim! His steps quickened and the closer we got to the attack site, the more animated and excited he became."

Upon reflection, Richard later said to me, "After I hiked in the Hayden Valley with you and saw the way you came alive, there's no question in my mind that's what you should be doing. You should be out in the woods studying the bears. That's your life, and if something happened to you tomorrow, you would have lived your life to the fullest."

We were about a mile and a half in when Richard asked, "How much farther?" I pointed to the only tree stand in sight, about a mile and a half to the west, and replied, "We need to go to the far left edge of those trees. That's what I did the last time and I need to hike to that point to get my bearings." In May, I had hiked around the swampy meadow before us. This time we plowed forward because this riparian zone was now dry as a bone.

Richard was beginning to understand how open this country was and became increasingly comfortable. He was content to be making far less noise than we did earlier. But because he was not in the kind of cardiovascular condition I was in, and he was wearing tennis shoes, hardly the ideal footwear for this terrain, we decided to split up for a short time to save him from walking the extra distance. My pace quickened as I headed due west, straight for the edge of the trees. Richard walked more to the southwest. I explained that we would not lose sight of each other out in the open and we'd meet up once I figured out my route from the day of the attack. I continuously looked back to keep tabs on Richard's position. He was traveling slowly but steadily with bear spray in hand and the safety off.

I reached my orientation spot, and after a time figured out what my path had been. It was actually an introspective process of getting into my own head to figure out what my thinking had been that day. What would I have done if I were me? The choice became obvious. Richard had disappeared from sight but reappeared just as rapidly none the worse for wear, and we reunited on the way to the fateful knoll.

An eerie feeling descended as we approached the notch while making plenty of noise. The area was far more open than I remembered. The distinct single line of sagebrush bushes looked smaller and more sparse than I had envisioned. I had no apparent reason to pay such close attention to all the details the first time. In hindsight, I obviously should have.

Every grizzly bear personality is different, and every encounter is different. In my particular confrontation, the mother bear acted aggressively to protect her cub. Was she unnecessarily aggressive? I don't believe so, nor do I blame her. For all I know, she could have had a hair-trigger reaction because she had lost cubs in the past. It was spring, shortly after cubs emerge from dens, and she had only one cub when the typical litter is two. It's not unreasonable to suppose that she had lost a cub or two fairly recently, or had a close call, but these are only possibilities and pure conjecture on my part.

It does serve to underscore the reality that no two bears behave in quite the same way. Like humans, some bears have more aggressive personalities, while I have been at close quarters with others that were incredibly calm in my presence. I do believe that in a similar situation most Yellowstone bears, even moms with cubs, would have fired off warning huffs or jaw pops or retreated completely, but that is also conjecture. However, my experience has taught me that, fortunately, most grizzlies do not show aggression toward humans unless they are surprised and feel threatened.

Still, I was voluntarily encroaching on the mother bear's turf, not vice versa. I certainly could have been making more noise. As you can imagine, I have replayed the incident over and over in my mind and the only thing I know for sure about what happened is that I will never know *why* it happened. Fortunately, life will go on.

We figured out how the ordeal had unfolded. As I had come down the knoll past the thin line of sage, there was a blind curve with a subtle but distinct depression. The mother bear must already have been in full defensive charge through this concavity toward an unknown threat before I sensed what was happening. She smelled and/or saw me long before I knew she was around. My fate might have changed only if I had been making lots of noise or carrying a can of bear spray with the safety off. Even then there were no guarantees, but I would have had a fighting chance.

Richard was astonished to be at the scene. He was also surprised that it had unfolded in such a wide-open area. I think he had imagined more of a forested scenario with dense cover. He told me that in this open a place, even he might not have been making much noise. It certainly did not look like a spot where a surprise grizzly bear attack would take place.

Richard was talking on his cell phone at the attack site when I decided to make a wide circle to look for spring carcasses and any other grizzly bear sign. Richard became more impressed with my hiking endurance when he saw me far away in one direction, then a few minutes later far away in another. It was like riding a bicycle; I was back.

Walking back and forth, I re-created my approach toward the charging mother bear several times in an attempt to analyze every aspect. Richard and I examined the various angles and snapped strategic pictures of the approach and the surrounding environment. Through this investigative process I realized that the vision in my right eye had improved more that I had realized. Even with one teary eye, my vision was clear. My appreciation for this magnificent landscape was heightened as never before. Richard said, "The billy goat is back." Indeed I was.

Richard was tuckered out and the shortest route out of here was the way we came in, but Richard had other ideas. He wanted to recreate my "hike for life" via Trout Creek. I was plenty satisfied that we had gotten to this point and had not thought of this, but what a great idea! However, I was seriously concerned that the hike would be too strenuous for Richard and he might have a real struggle on his hands to reach the road, but the old fart would have none of it. He insisted that we walk out the long way. The Yellowstone backcountry was not his element but he was determined to see this adventure properly through to the end.

It was a brilliant decision. I felt the terrain under my feet with unprecedented sensitivity. Even with only one eye, I had good vision. Richard was especially impressed when I spotted and described a northern harrier in the distance flying low over the sagebrush on the hunt for rodents. He has exceptionally sharp eyes and really appreciated my ability to see that kind of detail so far away.

I realized quickly that this hike to freedom was not as easy as I had imagined it. I visualized the route ahead as I always do. I stopped often to make logical route decisions as Richard followed. The more we walked the more that I was humbled and amazed by what I had done. As we hiked downhill along the southern perimeter of the transition zone hills, I further appreciated the difficulty of my escape. I must have wanted to live very badly, because this was ridiculous. My fitness and my footwear had saved my life. Had I not been in excellent physical condition, and had I been wearing tennis shoes like my pal the tennis teacher, I likely would never have made it.

We crossed trickling water a couple of times and each time Richard inquired, "Is this Trout Creek?" Each time I retorted, "No." We followed the valley's natural undulations while making our approach to Trout Creek. This is an area where John and Frank Craighead lived a good portion of their never-to-be-matched twelve-year grizzly bear study from 1959 to 1970. It was one of the most ambitious wildlife studies ever attempted. Combining their intimate knowledge and adventurous spirit with a brand new study tool, radio-telemetry, Frank and John uncovered vital information about the seasonal movements, social hierarchy, breeding and feeding habits, and life spans of grizzly bears. Despite fights with Washington bureaucrats, the federal government ultimately adopted many of their recommendations when it made grizzlies a threatened species under the Endangered Species Act in 1975.

As Richard and I followed the zigzagging waterway, we approached a major stretch with several tightly spaced, severe switchbacks. I knew that had been my escape path, right across the rushing water, photo equipment be damned. At this time of year the creek was relatively low, but it had been running high on May 23rd. Richard insisted that we ford the winding water the same way that I had done the first time. This fish out of water was determined to walk my path of survival and walk it he did. His attitude impressed me more than I can ever put into words. When the water rose up to his crotch during one of his creek crossings, he tossed me his phone and then his wallet as a couple of credit cards slipped out. I caught them cleanly, which impressed the hell out of him.

During this walk, I felt Hayden Valley's uneven terrain and plentiful pocket gopher holes with every step like never before. On the day of the attack, I never felt these bumps in the road. I had tunnel vision, relentlessly plowing and stumbling my way forward for as long as it took.

We reached the Grand Loop Road and took a few moments to look back and reflect. It took us almost two hours to get from the attack site to the road with clear vision; despite what I told the park ranger on the day of the attack, I really have no clear idea of how long the hike took after the mauling.

Richard puffed up the embankment to the Grand Loop Road and posed for pictures while holding on to the Trout Creek sign. He threw me the car keys then sat down in the turnout as I made a beeline for our car, a little over a mile away, where my faithful hound, Merle, was patiently awaiting our return.

Richard was physically spent and later said that it wasn't until I had walked out of sight that he realized that my vision was good enough to drive again. He had willingly handed over the keys without giving the matter much thought. I hadn't driven a vehicle since the morning of May 23rd. But two weeks before I left Boulder, I had two separate eye examinations. Dr. Durairlj and Dr. Hutchins both said that I would pass any driver's license test. The decision was up to me. Just two days earlier, I had mentioned driving to Richard and I thought he was going to come unglued. I could not go there, he said. I would surely be endangering other people. I respected his opinion, and his giving me the keys was clearly his tacit agreement that I was ready.

The fifty-two-mile drive back from Gardiner to Bozeman was easy, with a clear sky and the low afternoon sun at our backs. Richard made phone calls and was completely comfortable and relaxed as I cruised up Highway 89. This was easy stuff compared to all of my other trials and tribulations. We were smiling and laughing, reflecting on this landmark day, as we entered the Livingston city limits to fill up the gas tank. I was emotionally spent and a rejuvenated Richard took us home behind the wheel. No bears sighted, but what a day!

I had one remaining mission before I could consider moving on with the life that had been progressing before the mauling: I had to return to EIRMC. When they discharged me on June 2nd, I had told everyone that I would be back, and I meant it. I understand that ER and ICU personnel rarely see their patients again, presumably because people want to forget anything associated with such a traumatic time. I didn't want to be one of those people. A return to Idaho Falls was a major goal from day one.

My confidence increased after about a month of driving. Day by day, I picked up on the nuances of driving with one eye, such as swiveling my head around often to double-check my surroundings. My driving had been limited to necessary errands, mostly in the middle of the day when the traffic was light and the checkout lines were short. The drive from Bozeman to Idaho Falls would be about 300 miles each way with the entire route following Interstates 90 and 15. I was ready.

With the fall colors still brilliant but just past their peak, I relished this road trip—back in the saddle again. My arrival at the hospital on October 2nd in the late afternoon was quite emotional. The first landmark I spotted was the helicopter that shipped me here from West Yellowstone. I could only imagine what was happening during my flight for life while I was unconscious. I took a few pictures then proceeded directly to the emergency room. It was my intention to thank everyone who helped me in the ER but it was busy and I was unable to track down anyone who was present during my ordeal. I certainly didn't want to get in anybody's way.

My next stop was the ICU. When I told the two receptionists who I was, they personally escorted me up to the second floor. The ICU nurses let me right in and I jumped at the opportunity to walk around. I was eager to attach faces to the familiar voices.

Everyone in the ICU was so welcoming that I was a bit overwhelmed at first. I had a brief chat with Dr. Krell, who had monitored my recovery every day. I easily recognized his voice. He was pleased to see my great progress. After that I tracked down Robyn Meyer, an extraordinarily compassionate nurse who helped me so much. She was jubilant to see me. I asked her what kind of a patient I was.

Robyn said that we had a good working relationship. From her first time with me, she could tell that I wanted to do everything myself, and it was hard for me to accept that I couldn't. She noted that I exhibited patience with everybody but not with myself. She had helped to orient me to my new temporary surroundings and her presence gave me a comforting sense of continuity. Robyn explained that her style was to reason and compromise, but she told me "I never ordered you what to do. We discussed goals while I encouraged the best courses of action." We talked out each issue, built up mutual trust and understanding, both made compromises, but the decisions were ultimately left in my hands though Richard later told me, "What she said was the law."

Robyn made a point to express what a privilege this unscheduled reunion was for her because the nurses rarely see patients again after they are discharged. The warm conversation made me feel so good! We shared a long heartfelt hug and I promised to stop back the next day.

On the way out, I thoroughly inspected room 217, which was unoccupied on this day. It was nothing like I had visualized. This basic ICU hospital room had two sinks, two windows, a television, and was dramatically smaller than I had imagined. I noticed the reclining chair that had served as the bed for Ron and Richard as they alternated their nightly vigils. I was stockpiling goose bumps and my visit had just begun.

I stayed with Kim Wilkes, my former physical therapist, who was gracious enough to drive me to her house in the late afternoon so that I could become familiar with the route. I met two exuberant young dogs, Jackson and Murphy, a pure yellow lab and a yellow lab mix. They were gentle and friendly and I could immediately tell that we would enjoy each other's company over the next couple of days.

I was to meet Dr. Dan Hinckley at his office at 6 P.M. and I didn't want to be late. The door to his office was locked when I arrived a few minutes early. A cute little girl gazed at this eye-patched stranger from the other side of the glass entry door with a white lollypop stick protruding from the left side of her mouth. I identified myself to Dorothy, Dr. Hinckley's nurse, who had walked up from the hallway behind the blonde girl. Dorothy had just gotten off the phone with Dr. Hinckley and received word that he was on his way from the hospital, and due back at the office in a few minutes.

A bit later, a long, dark pickup truck pulled up near the back entrance to the building. Dan stepped out and cheerfully greeted me near the back of the office hallway. We shared a warm heartfelt handshake. It was a great moment. He was extremely pleased with my appearance and wore a broad smile. He took full-frame pictures of my face with his Nikon digital camera (something that has happened twice more since), and we were off to a restaurant.

We all had a warm, wonderful supper together. I talked a lot and ate slowly. Then Dan's wife, Jennifer, had to get to a meeting and he and I drove back to his office. Doctor and patient were talking up a storm by the time we pulled up to the back door of Dan's office. We walked into the empty building and sat on the couches in the waiting room. There were so many mysteries, so many questions to ask. My experience as an interviewer is limited and I really didn't know where to begin, but fortunately I had written down a comprehensive list of questions.

Dan told me that I had the most severe injuries he has ever seen from an animal attack. Another dubious distinction to add to my growing list. Dan has performed surgery on six other bear mauling victims, but I'm number one! I asked at what point he knew that I would survive. His response, "I never had any doubt you would live from the time we stepped into surgery." He said that my chest, abdomen, and brain were "all clear." In order to operate, he said he had to have all ducks in a row and "make sure that nothing was missed."

Closing my wounds, preventing infection, and preserving tissue was "like putting a jigsaw puzzle back together." All in all it took more than one thousand staples and stitches to put me back together. Then he said, "My religion is very important to me. I often feel guided in a case like yours where the amount of damage done is overwhelming. Just finding a place to start is a major accomplishment." I asked if anything would have been handled differently had he known what I looked like beforehand, even from a driver's license, and he said probably not, although it would have been "nice to have pictures."

Dan found no evidence that I was bitten on the back of the head, only raking claw marks. My injuries would have been far more severe, probably fatal, he said, if the bear had been biting my head or face with her canine teeth. The way the tissue was torn, I was raked one or more times across the face. Puncture marks on my left arm remained very tender for a long time, but this was apparently the only area of my body that was bitten.

I asked how I was able to keep track of the position of the sun. He explained that my right eye was never actually out of its socket like I had somehow perceived. My eyelid was, he said, "torn like a curtain and pulled apart. The eyelid was split away and you were looking out through a hole in that eyelid. Without that hole, you wouldn't have been able to see the sunlight that guided you out." This was sobering. That hole in my right eyelid was the slender margin between life and death.

Dan is a devout Mormon who always does what he feels is best for the patient as though he was treating and advising a close family member. No frills, blunt honesty, and what you see is what you get. He feels that Idaho Falls is a community where people really care for each other. Dan stated that many folks are drawn to the growing Idaho Falls area due to family values, and that this attitude positively affects the hospital care. From what I have seen, I can only agree wholeheartedly.

We talked for almost three hours. Normally I am very conscious of time, regularly peeking at my watch. When we finally stood up, I realized that I hadn't thought about my watch for the entire time that we were together. I thanked him again for saving my life, we shook hands, and I was out the door. But I knew I had a friend for life.

I wanted more answers about my time at EIRMC. I headed straight back to the hospital to check the ICU night shift for other nurses who had cared for me. Deb Lebel answered the ICU phone and pressed the magic button to open the big double doors. Deb's face lit up, beaming from ear to ear. She told me that my visit did the nurses as much good as it did me. I felt profoundly humbled and got a bit emotional. Then she came back with something like, "What do you expect in the middle of a potato field?" and we laughed.

As I rode the elevator down to the lobby, tears flowed freely. My emotions ran wild, bursting at the seams. I was laughing and crying at the same time. I made one more stop to look at all of the well-deserved awards on the wall again before exiting the hospital for the evening. I felt better than I had in a long, long time.

On my way to Kim's house, it dawned on me that this was the first time I had driven at night since I regained my driving ability. Thanks to Kim having shown me the way earlier, I had no problem and this further fueled my confidence. It was ironic that my first night drive happened to occur in Idaho Falls, a place I had never "seen" until this day.

An early morning shower, then self-acupuncture. Sticking needles in my body every day had become routine. Kim was about to leave for the hospital so I stepped out to say good-bye while showcasing my early morning acupuncture look. She got a kick out of this routine, just smiling and shaking her head, then she was off for the day. The Chicago Cubs were in the playoffs for the first time in a while and Kim, her husband,

Ed, and I planned to go out on the town tonight to watch the game at a local sports bar. Meanwhile, I had meetings with "Tall Paul," Dr. Durborow, and a few others.

Paul Thomas greeted me with a firm handshake and a warm smile at the main EIRMC entrance. He was pleased to see how good I looked and I proceeded to fill him in on what had transpired in my life since I left Idaho Falls. His goal had been to wean me into independence as quickly as possible and I was deeply grateful when I understood this. After a pleasant lunch at the famous Subway in the hospital, it was getting close to 1:00 and time to say farewell. We exchanged addresses and phone numbers and vowed to keep in touch. Paul made a point to ask me to say hello to Ron and Richard for him. We said our good-byes and it was on to the next event.

Stunning wildlife photography adorned the office of Dr. Catherine Durborow, located just around the corner from the hospital. She and her husband are avid wildlife photographers and travelers and she is a fellow University of Colorado alum who also happens to be an ophthalmic, plastic, and recon-structive surgeon.

Catherine beamed when she entered the patient room where I waited. We shared a warm hug. She explained her part in my surgery as: "Reconstruction of the right side of your face at the same time Dr. Hinckley worked on the left side." She told me that these were the worst injuries that she has ever seen. I was becoming accustomed to hearing this.

Dr. Durborow also took center stage in one of the most magical moments of my life: she entered room 217 one day to check on my eyes. Ron recalled, "Everyone around was nervous. Nobody knew what was going to happen." When she lifted up my right eyelid, I cried out with elation, "Oh my God! I can see!" However, I instinctively felt that my vision needed to be field-tested because nobody believed me. First I touched her hair and described it as bleached; no offense intended (remember, I was heavily medicated). Next I touched her necklace and described it. Then I touched and described her sweater. Apparently I was working my way downhill but Dr. Durborow remembered me saying, "I can't go any further." The nurse who accompanied her then chimed in, "Stop right there. You can keep your hands to yourself now."

All the folks in the room were happy and excited to witness this. Richard confided to me that even he had a tear in his eye, and tears don't come easily or often for him. He later described the event as "one of the most fun days of my life, really fantastic. That's a keeper!"

Slightly embarrassed, I asked Catherine if my vision test had crossed the line into "bad touching." Her response was a broad smile replete with giggles. "On the contrary! This was a great moment for me, too, and I tell the story often." Whew. I was off the hook.

Catherine needed to get to work but on the way out, she made a point to show me a framed image she took of a Kodiak bear with two standing first-year cubs. She described a third cub that was hidden from the camera by the high grasses, typical lush Kodiak vegetation during the long, rainy summers. We said our farewell as she walked directly into the room of a waiting patient. Catherine Durborow was the first person I saw after May 23rd. I will never forget that moment, and I doubt she will, either.

I made my way back to EIRMC and shared a final long hug with Robyn, with whom I had made a warm, wonderful connection. I also wanted to track down the guitar that Nancy Brown had found for me; I was quite attached to the instrument. My investigation brought me to the fifth floor, where I had spent my final three days after discharge from the ICU, and to a helpful lady at the front desk. To my surprise, she actually found a notation in the files about the guitar. She happily escorted me to the sixth floor office of occupational therapist Jim Crittenden. Sure enough, the very same guitar was situated straight up on the corner of his desk where I had left it last June with several signatures, including mine, on the aged wood top.

Jim told me with great pleasure that this old Stella Harmony guitar lived in this very spot in his office, intended for situations like mine. My guitar mystery was solved right away when I strummed a few chords and lead lines. The guitar was not hard to play. It was clear that my weakened condition back in May would have rendered virtually any guitar a challenge. The problem had been the guitar player, not the instrument.

My final stop was the helicopter landing pad, near where my van was parked. One of the pilots was there and I introduced myself and briefly recounted my story. As he opened up the side doors to give me a sense for what I had unconsciously experienced, I looked carefully and took lots of pictures.

The chopper was well organized, making excellent use of every inch of interior space. A team of three flew every rescue mission: the pilot, a medic, and a nurse. I imagined myself as the total focus of attention during my flight, lying on a stretcher, down for the count, flying over the scenic southwestern Yellowstone landscape.

This pilot was not the man who had flown me here. Each pilot is assigned a twelve-hour shift, similar to the nursing staff, and at least one pilot is on call twenty-four hours a day, seven days a week. "You never know when something will happen," he said. You've got that right. The previous day, he sat around through the entire shift with nothing to do. This morning, he had already flown two missions. I thanked him and while walking back toward my van, I watched an enclosed double golf cart vehicle tooling around the parking lot. It shuttles folks in need from their cars to the front door and vice versa. They really go the extra mile around here, I thought. I was proof of that. Finally, I got in my van for the drive back to Montana and my future. I had recovering to do, hikes to plan, a field season coming up, and a life to lead again. This time I knew for sure that I would come back to EIRMC again.

8

On a Personal Note

In some ways a man grows up quickly
In some ways he doesn't grow up at all
Oh how things would have been different for me
If my Dad like so many had died in the war

—"War Memories," music and lyrics by James R. Cole

M ANY PEOPLE HAVE ASKED me how I could stay so calm after my attack and why I have no fear about going back out among the grizzlies now, when I only have vision in one eye. I can only say that it seems to be the way I'm wired. But I can also say this: I have no such composure when it comes to the people dearest to me. When I spend time with the friends who were involved in my rescue and return to health, when I think about the family members I have lost who meant more to me than anything in the world . . . I can't help but be overcome with emotion. It's the people in my life who have enabled me to do what I have done in the past and to live my dream again going forward.

My father bequeathed to me many of the qualities that I think saved my life after mama bear left me alone and bleeding in the wilderness. He passed on his strong, sure legs—legs that I have used to hike thousands of backcountry miles. He taught me how to navigate in the dark, a skill that I'm certain helped me escape death. He helped to instill the love of the wild country in me with our cross-country road trips and nighttime drives searching for "eyes" of animals. And he passed along the sense of humor that I'm sure got me through some of the darkest periods after my rescue when I hallucinated, felt suffocating boredom, and wasn't sure I would see again.

I value my sense of humor above almost any other trait. I love to laugh, to listen to the unintentionally hilarious questions that children ask me, and to rib (and be ribbed by) my best friends. My entire family was funny, including my mother and sister. But nobody topped my dad. One day when I was a young pup, he wanted to see for himself if I could physically protect myself. Unsure, I dropped into an unrehearsed fighting stance. Dad had to restrain himself from doubling over. Suppressed laughter turned into a sideways smile, looking straight down to the floor. Chuckling, he looked me straight in the eye and said, "Don't fight, you'll lose. I'm just glad you have good legs."

I knew the right buttons to push and could always make my father laugh, whether it was over the phone or live and in person. He always played the part of Ralph when we mimicked routines from *The Honeymooners*. All I needed to say was "Cover your face Ralph," and he would be helpless.

Once when I was still in high school and Dad was out of town, his legendary good humor was tested. I borrowed his car to pick up my grandmother from the airport. But when I went looking for the car about an hour later, it had been stolen. A few days later, this time on my way to the airport (in a different car) to pick up my father, I contemplated how to break the bad news.

In the O'Hare terminal I performed a very brief soft-shoe comedy routine. As I danced with my arms out in front and to the side, I sang that immortal hit, "Da Da Da Da Da Da, The Cadillac Was Stolen." He immediately knew I was serious, but he laughed at my creative presentation. Insurance would cover the car. The only thing we lamented was the loss of our schnauzer Peppy's special dog dish, which had been on the floor of the back seat. My dad certainly enjoyed his automobiles and to him a Cadillac was symbolic of success. But he never lost sight of the big picture. He knew he was already a rich man. My father never lost his sense of humor.

Dad loved life more than anyone I've ever known (my hound dog, Merle, may be a close second). Road trips were one of the richest aspects of our life together, so when we found the time in March 1999 to do a California road excursion, it became the trip of a lifetime.

We visited Yosemite for a day and then drove on to the great golf courses of the Monterey Peninsula. Upon arriving in the early evening at our motel in Carmel, we noticed a poster for a whale-watching tour. One phone call and we were booked on the boat for the first expedition the very next day. The morning brought windy conditions with treacherous waves; the majority of the whale watchers on our boat spent most of their time staying dry inside the cabin. Not us. We were outside the whole time and had some whale sightings that most passengers missed.

From his naval experience, Dad knew how to anchor his legs on the wet deck while he held tight onto the rail. My seventy-seven-year-old overweight father was more stable than his lean, outdoorsy son. I was bouncing around like a yo-yo. "I've still got my sea legs!" he yelled through the wind and mist.

We staged an evening pinochle tournament on one of the beds of our motel room while sipping good vodka. (This is the same game I play with Ron with the famous opening bid of two-fifty.) It just doesn't get any better than that. We called Richard Berman that night just to share our joy. We spent most of the following day at the Pebble Beach Golf Links, one of the most famous public courses in the world. Dad and I staged our customary putting match on the Pebble Beach practice green and he beat my ass the same way he did in pinochle that night.

On Wednesday, March 10th, our golf clubs were already strategically situated in the trunk of Dad's classic Cadillac convertible, and we were off to our golf round at The Inn and Links at Spanish Bay, just north of Pebble Beach. We hadn't practiced at all and didn't expect much, but parts of the course ran along the Pacific Ocean and we knew this would be a fun outing. Dad had confided years before that he was living out his dreams, and I knew this trip was part of those dreams.

As I have already mentioned—and as I shared repeatedly with the ever-patient EIRMC staff—my father's golf round that day at Spanish Bay was the last of his life. But though his end probably came before it should have, in my mind he will always be the man who relished every bit of his life and was determined to live every minute of it on his own terms. I'm privileged to have shared much of it with him.

If Dad was the rock in my life, my sister was the sharp, crisp breeze. She remains one of my greatest sources of inspiration for the things that I do because she had a passion for the wild country—in particular, for Glacier National Park—that rivals my own. Her name was Linda Sue Cole, but to me she was Tootsie. I gave her that name after listening to the music of the great Al Jolson on our scratchy old Victrola. The Jolson recording of "Toot Toot Tootsie, Goodbye" was rolling around in my four-and-a-half-year-old brain when I began to sing it to my baby sister the first time I laid eyes on her the day she came home from the hospital. I looked into her big brown eyes and repeated, "Tootsie, Tootsie." I never addressed her any other way during her entire life.

Tootsie was a pistol from an early age, blessed with many talents. She was the fastest skater and runner in her age group throughout grade school, and a superb equestrian who at one time had a shot at the Olympics. Her spectacular chalk drawing of Nez Percé Indian Chief Joseph adorns the living room wall in my home in Montana. She also possessed an incredibly green thumb, and in the last years of her life she had her own developing landscaping business.

Though physically small, my little sister had a huge heart. I often let her beat me in sports, though she never caught on. She'd be so proud to hit the winning home run into the dog pen in our Chicagoland backyard after I set her up with a fat pitch. She was a lousy gin rummy player, but I would tank games just to see her radiant smile. Tootsie had a grin that would light up a room. Photos of her are all over the walls of my home and in each, you can see her sunny, fearless spirit shining through. Beating her big brother at anything boosted her confidence. Courageous and savvy, my baby sister never backed down from anything.

Throughout our lives, I could always make her laugh at will, taking great pains to do so with a well-timed punch line when she had a mouthful of food. She would invariably spit up her meal and we would laugh as we cleaned up the mess. Everyone should be so fortunate to laugh like that.

When she was all grown up, Tootsie came to live in Colorado, which put us blessedly close together. This was great fun. But after living in Colorado for close to ten years, she inexplicably moved back to Chicago, vowing to come back to the mountains with a stockbroker's license. It didn't seem like the right decision for her, but I think I know what her ultimate goal was: to follow her big brother and move back to the Rockies permanently with the means to make a living long-distance.

She adored coming out to Montana to hike with me in grizzly country. We shared many great backcountry adventures watching grizzlies in both Glacier and Yellowstone Parks. She was extremely confident and understanding about the bears and my passion for them, and I always enjoyed having her along. Glacier Park was her favorite place in the world, as it is mine. The two of us hiked and camped there for a week in August 2003. We plucked, picked, and consumed buckets of prime huckleberries through several days of arduous hiking on some of the most breathtaking trails you can imagine. "Not bad for a flatlander with bad knees," she said to me with that grin.

Tootsie was a wonderful sister and I can't imagine a brother and sister being closer. Once, when her children, Cara and Jeff, were battling as only siblings can, she shouted: "If you two were ever half as close as your Uncle Jim and I, it would be wonderful!" and then stomped out of the room. Despite her love for wildlife and the outdoors, she ended up marrying and settling down in suburbia, raising her children in Deerfield, Illinois. After her divorce, she and Molly Kiser (my wonderful Boulder nurse) had grand plans to move to Montana together after my nephew Jeffrey went away to college in 2008. Her game plan was to move to Bozeman and spend more time in Yellowstone and Glacier.

But it was not to be. Tootsie passed away from a lethal brain aneurysm eight months shy of her fiftieth birthday. Her sudden passing was difficult to believe and impossible to comprehend. I'm still not over it. No event in my life has ever affected me so deeply and for so long. I stand as the lone surviving member of my immediate family. I scattered my beloved sister's ashes in the Many Glacier Valley in Glacier National Park. Doubtless, brilliant flowers blossom each spring at that spot in her memory. She would like that.

It's odd how life works out. I've gained a new family since my attack, comprised of the people I only met after the fact who helped me survive and recover. Strangely, they are strung like pearls along the strand of Interstate 15: Dr. Hinckley in Idaho Falls, John and Judy Taylor in Pocatello, Judy Geiger (the nurse who rendered aid at the Trout Creek turnout) in Salt Lake City, and Kim Wilkes, the physical therapist, who now resides in Las Vegas. I could call them The I-15 Gang or something funny, but I'm honored to call them friends. My father and sister gave me my origins, but they gave me my future.

One of the most amazing things about meeting John and Judy Taylor was how I found them. I hadn't been able to find out who first helped me when I hiked out along Trout Creek, and that seemed like a missing piece of the puzzle that I might never locate. But as fate would have it, months after the attack, Judy went to see her doctor for a thyroid condition, and three guesses who her ear, nose, and throat specialist is? Daniel Hinckley. When she mentioned my attack, his receptionist gasped, "You're the missing link!" They, too, had been wondering about the people who found me, and here one of them was standing in their waiting area. It wasn't long before I was in touch with them. That story added to the "it was meant to be" feeling of our encounter.

When I asked Judy what it took for me to hike out, she said, "I think you clicked into a survival mode. That's when you go into yourself and you know you're here, and you have to get to there, and you do it." John added, "You knew you had to get out and your inner self drove you out. Your primordial self knows you have to survive and takes over. You could have just as easily gone right instead of left or west instead of east and wandered out there for hours and when they found you, you would have just been bones."

The Taylors have the spice of a long-married couple, and when they get rolling and teasing each other, they are hysterically funny. But they have also become lifelong friends and some of the finest people I know. Our first meeting was intense and emotional. "It was like closure," said John. "I'm still blown away by how calm we were. When we were directing traffic Judy hurt both her shoulders because she was waving them so fast to keep people from stopping. But the whole time we were controlled.

"We stopped at Three Rivers Ranch after we checked on you at West Yellowstone and fed the fish, and it was a catharsis," John continued. "We had seen the worst nature had to offer, and then we saw an osprey come in and swoop down and get a fish, and that was a very cleansing moment. We needed that for our own psyche." They stopped by EIRMC to see if I had made it and were told the minimum, which was all the hospital was allowed to share. They turned down the chance to do interviews with the press—"It was a very private thing," Judy said—and they went home. They didn't realize until later that

I didn't know who they were for almost a year. But I know now, and we'll be friends for the rest of our lives.

The other Judy in this story is terribly humble about her role in it, constantly saying that all she did was render a little first aid. To me, that's like Lindbergh saying, "I just took a little plane ride." Without Judy's assistance, I don't know if I would have made it to West Yellowstone, much less EIRMC. When we spoke after my recovery, she shared something amazing with me.

"On the anniversary date of your attack, my husband and I were in Yellowstone, and we actually saw you when we were in Hayden Valley," she said. "I told my husband, 'If you see an old green minivan, it could be Jim Cole.' We saw you the next day watching a mother bear and her cubs and I got out and told you I was Judy Geiger.

"I was surprised, looking at your face and what happened to your eye, that you could walk that far and have a sense of direction," she continued. "If you had taken one wrong step, you would have been coyote food. With the extent of the injuries to your face, I was surprised that you weren't drowning in blood going down into your lungs. But you were so coherent that when you got to the hospital I figured you would do okay. The doctors did a very good job on your face.

"It says a lot about the human will to live and ability to put the really bad side of things out of your mind so you can deal with your situation and get to where someone can help you. I was impressed."

Sitting in the living room of Dan Hinckley's magnificent

house overlooking the flatlands of Idaho Falls, I was struck once again by the calm of this man. He told me some harrowing stories about other people who had been attacked by bears and explained that my injuries had been far more severe than what he was used to seeing from an animal mauling.

"This was far beyond typical," he said. "Most of the (attacks) we get are not nearly this severe. The level of facial injury was as much as I've ever seen from a motor vehicle accident." EIRMC treats trauma from all over Idaho and Wyoming all the way down to the Utah state line, so Dan has seen plenty of facial damage and was well-equipped to repair mine.

"You left the hospital not being able to see anything, and for you to call and say, 'I can see and I'm comfortable driving down,' that was a major accomplishment," Dan said. Like most medical professionals, he doesn't get the pleasure of reconnecting with most of his patients, but we have become friends. "I've learned a lot more about bears talking with you, a lot more than is written in your two books," he continued.

Dan also concurs with the impression that Ron, Richard, and I got, which was that the type of personal care I received at EIRMC was truly exceptional. "I think people here in general are just very caring," he said. "I have a patient in the ICU right now and the nurse will call and ask me, 'Do you want me to go ahead and do this,' rather than waiting for me to ask. The nurses there are really something else; they really bond to people. They are always asking about you." True enough: each time I've gone back to visit, the faces of the nurses and staff light up like a Christmas tree when they see my mug.

I think it's because they don't get a lot of personal appreciation for the incredible work they do. Believe me, I appreciate it. I'm lucky beyond words to have had those nurses and Dr. Hinckley looking after me.

On the opposite end of the spectrum, we have the Park Service. I am honestly confounded by their attitude toward me. They have the potential to be part of the solution when it comes to protection of the grizzly bear and appreciation of the remaining wilderness in the Lower 48. Wouldn't you think that the Park Service would want to work *with* people like me and others who've spent a lot of time in Yellowstone and Glacier, particularly in the backcountry? Why not leverage our experience and knowledge to educate people about the wonders of these incredible places?

When I first moved to the area back in 1998, within a year I went to their bear management people and offered to help them gather information about grizzly bears for free. They don't have people in the field doing much of this, in part because of lack of manpower. But they turned me down flat. They had no interest in working with me, even though I had done mountain lion research there and worked with the Park Service in the past.

After my attack in 2007, the Park Service officer who was onsite and filed the official report confiscated my camera equipment, cell phone, and computer to use as proof against me for what they assumed was the crime of getting too close to a bear in order to take photos. The press release the Park Service issued later that day was inaccurate. They assumed I had been taking pictures of bears when in fact I hadn't even seen any bear sign prior to being attacked. When they got a warrant and inspected the flash card from my camera, they found not a single photo of a grizzly. But the assumption was still incorrect. No correction or retraction was ever offered.

When Ron and Richard went to recover my possessions while I was still in EIRMC, the Park Service gave them a hard time. "I was also working to get some of Jim's stuff back from the Park Service, because they had impounded his vehicle," Ron said later to Tim Vandehey. "Rich and I actually drove down to Yellowstone and got some of his things, but they wouldn't release his camera or his computer. They wouldn't release his cell phone. I told them Jim had a voice activated cell phone and he had no use of his eyes and needed to call people. But they wanted to keep it because they said Jim could have taken photos of bears with it. The guy's a professional photographer—why would he use his phone to take pictures?

"Jim didn't want his camera equipment sitting in an evidence locker somewhere and getting stolen or busted," Ron continued. "It was ridiculous that they wouldn't release something like that. He wanted his journals and they wouldn't let him have them. What were they afraid of, that he'd written a journal entry about the attack?"

I don't understand why it has to be this way and I wish things could be different. I think there are a lot of great, dedicated people working for the Park Service. We could do so much together with their resources and my knowledge. Imagine a kind of Grizzly Conservation Corps of college students

JIM COLE WITH TIM VANDEHEY

going into the wilderness for a week and studying the bears and their habitat. Imagine what the Park Service and I could accomplish together. Unfortunately, for now, that remains just in my imagination.

Finally, we come to Richard and Ron. Their love and commitment to me was my anchor during those first dark, disorienting days at EIRMC. Their chatter about pinochle hands and White Sox baseball pulled me out of a deep hole, and they had the incredible patience to listen to my ceaseless banter at a time when I think the rest of the people in the ICU were ready to stuff a sock in my mouth to get some silence.

Richard and I have had our conflicts over my work with grizzlies. He thinks what I do is dangerous and that my attitude toward the bears is irresponsible. I disagree. We respect each other's opinions as friends must, but it's a subject we generally avoid because there is no reconciling our views. Still, I respect his passion and that it comes from an honest desire to see me safe, healthy, and happy.

"Jim is exactly the same guy he was before the mauling," he said in a later interview with Tim. "I think he's the only guy in the world who's been mauled twice who hasn't learned a damned thing.

"He has a unique ability to tell a story that maybe nobody else ever has been able to tell," Richard continued. "For him, it's his hope to have a venue where people will learn about the great bear in ways they never could have heard via the media. Because of the attack and the attention, he now has an opportunity to share what he knows about the bear with a mass audience. When Jim is in front of an audience, singing songs, answering questions, and telling stories, he's engaged, he's in his environment as much as when he's in bear country. He's engaging, gregarious, a showman . . . he's like Will Rogers.

"As far as the way we disagree," Richard continues, "we could be together for days and the bear isn't brought up. When he respects that he's not going to talk me into being comfortable in bear country, we're very copacetic. Jim is a mensch. He is really a good human being."

Ron is more understanding of my grizzly-loving ways and tolerates my eccentricities the same way that Richard does . . . the way that lifelong friends tolerate each other. His family is another story. "Everybody in my family thinks he's nuts," Ron said in the interview. "But I think his recovery is amazing. He went out there to the site on the one-year anniversary, and he was out there again on the two-year anniversary. He sent me the first photo of a grizzly bear that he took after the attack, which was in the same area: off at a distance, blurry, not a great shot. But for him it was a milestone.

"Plenty of people think he's nuts," he continues. "I sometimes question it. But it's his passion. He says he has no fear. I haven't been out with him, and I think he'll be a little more cautious, but he still wants to praise the bear so that people understand it and don't walk around in fear of it. I'd like to see him live a less solitary lifestyle and come back to Chicago for more visits, but this is what he does. He loves the time outdoors, then once he gets back, he loves documenting it. And he sings about it—it's like a mix of Arlo Guthrie and Bob Dylan."

Everybody's a critic. But I think I'll let Richard have the last word on my questionable virtues. "Jim's life is incredibly simple. He can live on very little, his needs are simple, and his wants are simple. He has a very simple existence that makes him happy."

Couldn't have said it better myself, brother.

The people of EIRMC are precious to me, and it was with delight that I made another trip back to see them on January 17, 2008. I returned to Idaho Falls a second time to speak at a community event celebrating the hospital's verification as Idaho's only Level Two Trauma Center, one of only 113 in the country. This was a big deal. Folks around Idaho Falls are active in hunting, rodeo, skiing, and climbing and don't mind taking a few chances in their spare time. Some foolhardy folks have been known to drive snowmobiles in excess of a hundred miles per hour, running the risk of surprising a moose or a herd of elk around a blind curve. A Level Two Trauma Center handles the direst cases and must be up to the challenge.

After the social hour, where everyone enjoyed drinks and goodies, four speakers addressed the crowd from a spotlighted, makeshift podium: Doug Crabtree, CEO of EIRMC; Jared Fuhrman, mayor of Idaho Falls; Brian O'Byrne, M.D., EIRMC Trauma Medical Director; and Jim Cole, former patient. I was honored and I let the crowd know how I felt about the people of the hospital. It was incredibly emotional for this big softie. I told some memorable stories from my eleven days in their care, and when I publicly thanked Dr. Hinckley, the mere mention of his name drew a standing ovation.

Several nurses who were present in the ER when I first arrived introduced themselves. One ER nurse with a brand new baby confided that her initial reaction was, "How did he walk out?" Others told me they were amazed at my fortitude. The entire evening was a warm, welcoming lovefest. I ate it up.

The Community Relations Department presented me with a heartfelt card that reads as follows:

Thank you so much for coming all the way out here to help with our event at the hospital. Having you share your story adds so much to our celebration. Your presence provides the "reason why" we do what we do here at EIRMC. We wish you all the best as you continue to heal and go on with your life. Take care.

9

Why I Still Love the Grizzly

Land of plenty, land of gold
Eden, a paradise, memories grown old
This hallowed soil meant for all to share
Forsaken land of the Golden Bear
Forsaken land of the Golden Bear

—**"Land of the Golden Bear," music and lyrics by James R. Cole**

EVERYBODY HAS HIS OWN cross to bear. It's 2009 as I'm working on this book, and now that life is slowly starting to resemble the life that I had before the mauling, I find myself reflecting on what has changed, what hasn't changed, and what it all means. My face remains a work in progress—something that old friends like Richard insist was the case even *before* the attack. As I write this I've had one more complicated surgery to reshape the left side of my face, straighten my nose and solve a problem with my good eye. My nose is looking a bit more like its old self, but my eye still blurs with tears, making driving at night, looking downward, and reading fine print tougher. My nose, most of my upper lip, and a substantial portion of the left side of my face and head are numb. That will not change, and I have accepted it.

Otherwise, I'm in great shape. I was never much of a weightlifter in my younger days; I was the cardiovascular wild man who could hike twenty-five miles with a heavy pack or run around a tennis court all day without getting winded. Lean as a greyhound with the strong legs handed down by my dad—that's how I've almost always been, despite an insatiable, lifelong lust for food that I still battle. But because of a torn rotator cuff that occurred during the mauling, and after learning a weightlifting routine from my physical therapist, I started working on my upper body. Now I have made the acquaintance of pectorals, biceps, and deltoids I didn't even know I had.

I'm probably the strongest I have ever been right now, at sixty years old. I'm currently in as good a shape as I've ever been. My overall health will never be 100 percent, but 80 or 90 percent isn't bad and I'm ecstatic about life. By late June 2009, when I was completing the first draft of this book, I'd already hiked more than 1,500 miles for the year. It keeps me young. That feels good, because I intend to be going out into the field, walking in grizzly country, for many years to come.

Emotionally, I'm as good as ever. As I discussed, when I was mauled in 1993, I had no emotional fallout. After this attack, I had that one night in the hospital where I relived the attack, and that was it. In contrast, I had nightmares every night for a month or two and lingering, disturbing dreams for about a year after my father died in my arms. However my mind works, those are the facts. I can't imagine being as emotional about anything as I was (and sometimes still am) about my father collapsing and never speaking another word. I'm an emotional man about the people in my life and the relationships that are my anchor, but anyone who was expecting me to have flashbacks or break out into a cold sweat the first time I slipped backpack straps over my shoulders is going to be sorely disappointed.

I have done everything in my power to get my life back and do as much or as little as I choose. Obviously, with the loss of an eye, some of my activities have had to be modified, but I'm stubborn enough to fight to get back to where I was, as any of my nurses or physical therapists can tell you. In the 2009 field season, I made it a point to do everything that I normally do in the field: including hiking Yellowstone, finding the mother bear who attacked me, and getting a decent picture of her and her yearling cub. I'll never know for sure if she was the one who mauled me, but I'm 95 percent certain. No harm, no foul. She was just being what she was in the same way I'm being what I am.

I've taken the same trips to Glacier and into the backcountry of Alaska that I did before the attack. On those trips, what came home to me was that even having only one eye, I didn't feel less comfortable around the bears. As I said before, my savvy and experience made up for my loss of vision. When I went back for my fortieth high school reunion, I played base-ball and hit left-handed, and all the instincts were there. I'm not going to make anybody forget Rod Carew, but I didn't em-barrass myself. When I drive, I have limited depth perception, so I have to be extra careful not to run into something or someone that I can't see, particularly at night. But in general, life goes on, and that sure beats the alternative.

It is my fervent hope that this book serves as another ex-ample of an inspirational fight for the most precious gift we all have, our lives. I appreciate from the bottom of my heart the outpouring of cards, letters, flowers, gifts, and calls I have re-ceived from people all over the country. I am humbled by all of the caring, compassion, and, most of all, love that I have ex-perienced during this stressful time, but I do not want anyone to feel sorry for me. Though I had never given it any thought, Richard later told me, "You never complained once from the moment you awakened in the hospital. You never said why me, why me, no complaints, remorse, or woe is me. After all you went through, then three months at my house, you never complained."

Why didn't I bemoan my physical challenges? I think part of it is because of a realization I've held onto for years: my life is good, really good; I'm living a dream that many others would love to be living and I accept the risks. I don't kid my-self that millions of Americans are dying to live a Spartan life in Montana and spend half of their time tramping about the wilderness carrying the equivalent of a four-year-old child on their backs. But millions of people dream of getting out, dropping out of the rat race, and chasing their passion; but because of money, commitments to family, or other reasons, most never do it. I've been blessed enough to live a life that makes me wake up each morning excited just to be drawing breath. I suppose even when I was attacked, part of me knew that my encounter with that mother grizzly was just another organic, natural part of that life.

I am certainly no hero. All I did was save my own skin. Dr. Hinckley is a hero in my mind, and not just for patching me up. Ron and Richard will always be my heroes; there aren't enough superlatives to describe how I feel about those two characters. They literally put their busy lives and careers on hold to be by my side, step by step, during my entire recovery period in Idaho Falls. It is a gift beyond belief to have friends like this. Richard and Ron are the two most unselfish individuals I have ever known. If there's a final hero in this drama, it's my father, who showed me the way by following his dreams and teaching me how to be strong and love everything about life, even the rough parts.

As for the meaning of what happened to me, that's as much a work in progress as my face. I think about what I've endured and think about how to lend some sort of meaning to it, and great Cubs third baseman Ron Santo comes to mind. I'm a Chicago sports fan after all, and though I've always been a White Sox guy, you have to admire Santo. He played the great game with exuberance every day during his illustrious fifteen-year career, despite being diagnosed with juvenile Type One diabetes at age eighteen and given a life expectancy of only twenty-five years. He became captain of the Cubs and was a nine-time all-star. What impresses me is that he kept his condition a secret for the first twelve years of his career because he wanted to be treated as an equal, not to be discriminated against or given a break due to his disability. Santo courageously played with various injuries, rarely missed a game, and, to this day, stands as the only position player in major league baseball history to play with this deadly disease—and oh, how he played.

My point is, Ron Santo has lived his life with courage and given it meaning by what he has done. At this writing, he has been battling diabetes for close to fifty years and despite being a double amputee, he has an incredibly positive attitude toward life. As an exuberant radio broadcaster for his beloved Cubbies and an activist for diabetes research, he has helped raise over $50 million for the Juvenile Diabetes Research Foundation. That is how you lend meaning to misfortune: you find a way to turn it around and make it into a way to bring good fortune into the lives of others, whether it's by inspiring them, educating them, raising money, or changing policy.

I found the meaning in what happened to me when I went back out to the attack site, then later when I went back out to Glacier and up to Alaska in October 2008. I realized that the meaning in the attack lay in the opportunity it created for me to write this book and gain greater visibility as an educator, so that I can teach more and more people about the truth of the grizzly bear and its endangered habitat. Without the drama inherent in the attack and its aftermath, I would have continued writing songs and speaking at schools and other forums, but it would have been far more difficult to gain a national audience.

Now, because of what seemed on the surface to be a tragedy, I have a chance to reach tens or hundreds of thousands of people with the message that grizzlies are complex, mysterious, and unspeakably beautiful—and that their health mirrors our own futures as inhabitants of the same natural world. In a very real way, the attack has made it possible for me to fulfill my life's purpose in a way that would not have been available to me before.

I keep writing songs about the bears, and I've even written a song about the incident itself. As you read this, I will have been released from seclusion; I was forced to put a moratorium on my school appearances so I could keep the high-drama details of my attack and survival under wraps until the book came out. That was difficult. I love speaking to kids and enlightening their parents, and I adore getting up in front of a crowd with my guitar and getting them to sing along with my songs about the grizzlies. That is my drug of choice. Now that my embargo has been lifted, I'm free to talk to students, adults, and the news media about what happened to me and to resume spreading the truth about the grizzly bear. I hope that I'm having an impact on attitudes and helping to foster less fear and more wonder about them.

Nothing could have prepared me for the way people stare at my facial appearance, especially children. That hasn't been easy, but I often break the ice with curious youngsters by saying hello. At first, I was a bit tentative but I've gotten used to being the eye-patched pirate, and I no longer feel uncomfortable in the role. The first time a child asked if I was a pirate, I said, "Yes, isn't today Halloween?" The young boy cocked his head with a bemused look as his mother smiled. That's a standard line for me now. There's no reason for me to hide. What happened to me happened, and I don't use it as an excuse or apologize for it. As my dad used to say, "Take me as I am or don't take me."

These days, when I'm not out in the field, I'm in public as much as possible, in big venues and small ones, on local platforms and national ones, teaching. Not just about the grizzly bear, but about life. I hope I can inspire people about life in general and how precious it is. I want to help people, who might not go through something as traumatic as I did, to cherish life all the more. This is especially important with the brutal economic times that we went through in 2008 and 2009. A lot of folks lost everything they had, and many of those who didn't had their lives irreversibly changed. For a lot of people, that's depressing. But my implied message is that no matter how bad things may seem, you can always make a comeback as long as you don't lose faith in yourself. Life may not go back to the way it was (it could never be the same) but that doesn't mean it can't be a new world for me, and even better than before.

I'm delighted to be back in the schools. These days, I

might speak and sing in a large concert hall and then go into a schoolroom with twenty kids. I don't care. Kids are the future of the grizzly bear and they are my most important audience. It is critical to reach them at a formative age and help them acquire a love and awe and understanding of nature, so when they become adults they will want to preserve what little wilderness we have left. Research suggests that if children do not connect with nature before they are eleven years old, they are far less likely to travel to natural places and work to protect them from development when they grow up.

I'm also answering a lot of questions about myself, my attitudes toward the bears, and my actions in the wild. Since my attack, a number of people both online and offline have expressed the opinion that I brought it on myself because I was "harassing the bears." One of the things I do in my speaking is dispel this myth about how I conduct myself in grizzly bear country. Let me say this: I don't approach bears inappropriately. I position myself according to the situation; I read the bear's activity and body language and position myself to observe and hopefully photograph.

I can't say I never disturb a grizzly, but it's rare and I am very careful about it, because my goal is to document what they are doing naturally, not how they're reacting to me. When a mother bear nurses at my feet, when cubs come up to check me out with no aggression, when wild bears do a host of things that most people wouldn't believe, the difference between me and other people is that I understand bear behavior and keep my cool. Most people would react with submission, panic, or fear or do something that could create a problem. My policy is simple: don't approach or disturb. I'm deeply conscientious about it. Still, I don't recommend what I do to anyone. It takes experience and a great deal of discipline to minimize the dangers to humans and bears.

The issue of bear spray is a perfect example. Although everyone who ventures into grizzly country should be armed with bear spray, it likely will never be needed. My attacks both happened so quickly that my spray never left the holster. However, in most scenarios, a person spots or hears the bear first and usually has enough time to pull out the spray and discharge it if necessary. The spray has proven to be highly effective in most situations when properly deployed. The trouble is that many people who should carry it don't, and that creates danger not just for humans but for the bears.

On September 9, 2007, Yellowstone National Park safety officer Ken Meyer was mauled by a female grizzly accompanied by her two cubs just north of the park near Gardiner, Montana, early in the morning while on a legal black bear hunt. He, of all people, was not carrying bear spray. Meyer apparently chose to fight the protective mother bear instead of lying still and acting nonthreatening. According to reports, he apparently kept moving toward his rifle when the mother bear retreated, and she may have perceived this as ongoing aggressive behavior. I do not want to overspeculate because I wasn't there. But apparently when the dust settled he planted a shot in the mother bear, then walked back to his vehicle and drove himself home to Mammoth Hot Springs with severe injuries.

The area of the attack, near Gardiner, was closed to the public out of concern that the wounded bear might be dangerous if still alive. The closure was lifted after the mother bear's body was finally located on October 4th with the bottom part of her jaw shot off. Her two orphaned cubs were apparently seen wandering through the general vicinity.

In effect, Meyer probably killed three grizzlies with his reactive behavior, particularly if the cubs were in their first year of life. It's doubtful that they would have been able to survive on their own. What does his behavior say to park visitors? Why didn't he carry bear spray? It appears that Meyer did not play dead, a basic strategy for surviving a grizzly attack, and so violated one of the most important safety protocols.

Ken Meyer is lucky to be alive. So am I. I do not carry nor have I ever owned a firearm, so his defensive choice would never be an option for me, nor should it be for anyone truly interested in seeing the great bear in its natural surroundings. Remember, we all venture into the grizzly's domain voluntarily. If I had attempted to fight back during either of my two attacks, the already-angered bears could have become even more provoked and I may not have lived to tell the tale. Even a "small" grizzly is far superior to a grown man in strength, speed, and ferocity, so attempting to fight back is utterly futile. The reason the bear in Hayden Valley did not kill me on the spot was because the attack was defensive; as soon as she was sure I no longer posed a threat to her cub, she was out of there.

Of all the people who should know to carry bear spray, it's hunters who should. But only some do. On September 14, 2007, a bow hunter was calling in elk when he was attacked and injured by a female grizzly with three cubs just north of Yellowstone in the Beattie Gulch area. Not having brought bear spray, he attempted to climb a small tree to safety, but the bear "ripped the tree in half and pulled [him] down with it." When he hit the ground, the man finally did something right by playing dead. This action probably saved his life.

Another bow hunter was mauled by a grizzly bear with three cubs in this same area on October 6th, prompting the second closure of the Beattie Gulch area in three weeks. The guy was hunting with two friends and according to Mel Frost, a spokesman for the Montana Department of Fish, Wildlife and Parks, "Nobody had bear spray. It's something we can't emphasize enough. He remembered to play dead, so she bit on him and left. One of the hunters shot at the bear, but there's no evidence the bear was hit."

At least two other bow hunters were mauled during the same hunting season in the fall of 2007. A grizzly attacked a bird hunter who didn't have bear spray on October 15th on the Rocky Mountain Front. During that year's legal fall hunting season, grizzly/hunter encounters forced closures in several other wilderness areas.

So we have a grand total of five hunters who were mauled by grizzly bears in 2007. What's important to remember is that at least one bear died as the result of all this—but zero humans died. Hunters walk a tightrope because they wear camouflage and try not to make noise, thus increasing their odds of a surprise bear encounter. As far as anyone knows, none of the hunters I listed above carried bear spray, a foolish breach of basic bear country safety measures. Yet they all escaped with their lives. This result says as much about the bear as it does about us. It says that we're lucky the grizzly takes such a simple, straightforward approach to the threat posed by humans: neutralize the threat, then get the hell out of Dodge.

Some people have accused me of anthropomorphizing the bears, making them out to be cute and curious teddy bears when in fact, in the minds of most people, they are unstoppable, unknowable predators. The fact is, they are neither. I have never humanized grizzlies, because that disrespects the great animals. They are not amusement park animatronics, and the grizzlies that cause the "bear jams" in Yellowstone were not put there for the pleasure of visitors. When you stop respecting the grizzly bear, you become part of the problem, because you either don't take precautions in the wild and set yourself up for problems, or you don't take preventive steps in areas near bear country and invite a bear intrusion that can end with a dead bear. The bottom line is that grizzly bears—and every other powerful creature, from the bison to the wolf—should be treated with a mixture of awe, admiration, and reverence. At the end of the day, grizzly bears are wild animals. We should never try to be pals with the grizzly, just have a peaceful coexistence.

At some appearances, a few people outrightly tell me that I'm a fool. They ask incredulously, "How can you go out there among grizzly bears? You actually *look* for the bears!" Well, I'm not interested in just a hike. I've hiked thousands of miles in Rocky Mountain National Park but it doesn't hold my interest because it doesn't have grizzlies. What I tell them is this: aside from the fact that I know how to handle myself in bear territory, when I am in grizzly bear country, I'm at home. I feel free and completely at peace. I can't wait until the snow is gone so I can hike into the backcountry. I'm a different person when I'm there. It's the same way as soon as you put a microphone and a crowd in front of me.

My goal is to dispel myths about the wilderness and the bears—especially that it's unsafe to hike in grizzly country. Seeing someone with a face that looks like mine, caused by a grizzly, might make that harder at first. But none of this has shaken my trust in the grizzly bear. If anything it is greater than ever. That sounds funny to my audiences when they look at my face, but I remind them to keep things in perspective. My risk of being attacked is greater because I probably spend more time alone in grizzly habitat than any person alive; it's a numbers game. But no part of life is without risk. I still feel safer in bear country than in big cities. In my photographs and stories, I'm showing the peaceful side of the animals (which is about all I ever see) and showing what is possible.

Ron and Richard have accused me of downplaying the hike

to survival. I'm not. I simply had no choice. My options were limited and I fought for my life with everything I had. Hiking out from this incident was the hardest thing I've ever done in my life and I'm lucky and grateful to be alive.

I'm a marathoner, not a sprinter. You may beat me in the short term but I'm in it for the long haul and I will never quit. I've worked hard to get my life back but as expected, it hasn't been easy. Early on during my physical and emotional healing process, the simplest tasks took on monumental proportions. Now life is about as close to normal as it will ever get. Normal is good, whatever that means, but it's the struggles in life that teach us the most valuable lessons.

It may sound silly, but I'm grateful for the entire painful process that has been my life's journey for these past three years. I have gained valuable new perspectives on life that were never a possibility without experiencing extreme hardship. I was forced to confront my own emotional abyss and face feelings that I had never come close to before and probably would never have dug up in the first place. My forced time away from the world, my home, and my dog have magnified my appreciation for the little things in life that we take for granted all too often. I relish going to sleep in my very own bed, a kitchen with a full-sized refrigerator, the taste of a healthy meal I've cooked fresh for myself, my office, a lifelong accumulation of reference materials, pictures of family and friends, family heirlooms and memorabilia, the sound of a baseball game on the radio on a summer evening, and simple peace of mind.

It's as though I know finally that everything is all right in the moment, and that the moment is enough. No one who hasn't experienced a shattering, perspective-changing setback can imagine what it means to look at the most mundane aspects of life as if they were alien artifacts that suddenly dropped out of the sky.

When I came home after a hard recovery, I dreaded dragging myself out into the wilderness to break trail in fresh snow after a winter storm. "Let somebody else break trail" became a convenient excuse to be lazy and take the day off. No big deal. The next day would be easier skiing in somebody else's tracks. But when I got out there, I realized I had forgotten how wonderful it is to be the first one on the trail at first light, whether trudging through deep powder or gliding through an inch or so of white silken ground cover, where tracks are clear and easy to read. These are the kind of winter mornings that I've lived for, yet my injuries robbed me of them for a time. Regarding them with fresh eyes (or eye, to be accurate), I saw how precious they were.

For the rest of that winter, I reveled in reading animal tracks in the snow more than I had in a long time. One morning I was hot on the tracks of the pair of coyotes I mentioned in the Introduction. They had intercepted a young moose. I read the story in the tracks: the moose's lengthened stride indicated a short sprint then a sharp cut down a precipitously steep slope, finished by a vanishing act into the dense timber down below. I didn't see any of these animals on this day, but their story was crystal clear to me in the fresh snow.

During the past two winters, I have proven to myself that

I can still take photographs with the best of them, even with only one eye at my disposal. In the Gallatin National Forest, I chronicled the late winter activities of a mother moose, accompanied by her handsome yearling calf. Only a mile from my house, I took wonderful shots over a three-day period of five bald eagles competing for their fair share of a road-killed deer carcass.

In early May, a mother bear showed up in Mary Bay in Yellowstone with three spring cubs. She was a well-seasoned mom and I had watched her raise other litters in this area for years. I have no idea what happened but sometime that spring, two of the cubs got separated from her and she was traveling the area with only one. I had spotted one of the separated cubs cross the road near Fishing Bridge a few days before and others had reported seeing the tiny wayward cubs without their mother. Since all four bears had remained in the same general area, I was hopeful, but not particularly optimistic that they would reunite. As I have mentioned, after my fateful Hayden Valley hike I planned to drive back to the area to try to keep tabs on this continuing drama.

Exactly one year later to the day later, on my first extended trip into the field after the mauling, I was thrilled to see the mother bear foraging in Mary Bay with two yearlings. She had found one of the missing cubs last spring, but not the other. Though I was sad that the third cub didn't survive, I was ecstatic for the two that did. Given the natural mortality rate for first-year cubs, the mother bear earned high marks. Subsequently in May 2009, I saw this same mother grizzly with two healthy two-year-olds. They would likely soon be on their own but this great mother bear had done her job and I was grateful to be alive to see the result.

One thing has not changed at all: almost every day I wake up at about 5 A.M., needing no coffee, just excited about life. Some feeling has come back to the left side of my face and mouth, due primarily to some natural healing and the effects of my year of self-administered daily acupuncture. My whistling skills have returned after a one-year hiatus. I can't wait for each day. Many evenings, just before going to bed, I watch an episode or two of *The Honeymooners* because their familiar routines always make me laugh. I know every episode by heart; it's still the funniest television show ever made. Even my nighttime siestas now feel like productive, soulful, unconscious meditative states of being. I really can't explain it.

I know that going forward, my path is to slowly pare back my time in the wilderness with the bears and ramp up my time educating, singing, and speaking. That's better than fine; this is the right time to move on to that next stage of life for me. Everything is peace; everything has meaning. It may seem very odd to read this from a man who had half his face ripped off by a bear while losing the sight in one eye, but to paraphrase another of my heroes, Lou Gehrig, I feel like the luckiest man on the face of the earth.

The only shadow in my mind comes from the grizzly bears in particular and our wild lands in general. These are pivotal times for our environment. The year 2008 was a catastrophic year for the grizzly bear. In Yellowstone country, the government estimates that seventy-nine grizzly bears died in 2008 due to human-related causes (primarily being killed by hunters or destroyed as "nuisance bears" after being attracted to garbage), the highest mortality rate ever recorded. There are likely many more we don't know about. It's not a coincidence that April 2007, the U.S. Fish and Wildlife Service removed Endangered Species Act protection for the Yellowstone grizzly. This suggested that all was well with the creature at the top of the food chain and virtually gave carte blanche to hunters to pop away at the great mammals without repercussion, which they did in 2008.

This disaster was compounded by the effects of climate change: specifically, the massive die-off of white bark pine trees, whose nuts are a critical fall food source for the bears. The warm winters and drought conditions of the past ten years allowed mountain pine beetles to decimate the trees at elevations where they wouldn't have ventured in past years due to colder temperatures.

On April 15, 2009, the agencies responsible for administering the U.S. Fish and Wildlife grizzly bear policies in Yellowstone met in Bozeman to discuss Yellowstone grizzly mortality. In their language, the shocking rise in dead bears was a "spike"; I would call it a calamity and a portent of things to come. Agency officials said they planned to reduce future deaths with improved hunter education, requiring wider use of bear spray, and by launching a limited grizzly bear hunt in Montana, Wyoming, and Idaho, which to me is like trying to lower flood waters by breaking a levee on the assumption that the water will flow *out*. The people at this meeting pointed out that the grizzly population in the Greater Yellowstone Ecosystem, currently estimated to be about 600, is larger than it was in the early 1970s, but that's not the point.

The combination of delisting of grizzlies, the radical changes in the ecosystem wrought by climate change, and the effect of minimally regulated hunting suggests one thing to me: the current methods and mindset of the U.S. Fish and Wildlife Service are not sufficient to manage this situation and protect the grizzly bears or other alpha predators. Things are changing in the Mountain West: more people are moving in, the weather is becoming warmer and drier, and political pressures are mounting to open up areas for energy exploration. New thinking is required, not just a retooling of old policies.

There is some new thinking going on, as well as some hopeful action. A project is underway to educate people on protecting the few remaining grizzlies in the northern Cascade mountain range, a population that has dwindled to about ten. In May 2009, a new federal plan was proposed that would close hundreds of miles of backcountry roads to motorized vehicles in the Selkirk and Cabinet mountains, which cross western Montana and eastern Idaho. The proposed Selkirk and Cabinet-Yaak Recovery Zones would exist for one main reason: to protect grizzly bears. That's encouraging.

One of the most hopeful signs for the future came when I finally went back to performing at schools. Prior to the mauling, I spent a substantial amount of time presenting grizzly bear education programs at elementary schools. I love working with children and their unbridled enthusiasm. They ask the best questions, and since they will be the future caretakers of the great bear, I'm happy to provide answers.

Many elementary school classes have sent me "thank you" packets with heartfelt cartoon drawings and notes, but there was something extra special about the pictures I received from LaMotte Elementary School in (appropriately) Bear Canyon near Bozeman. Those kids remembered my words better than I did. Some of their drawings depicted the real-life grizzly bear characters from my slide shows: Snaggletooth, Diver, Bullitt, and The Runt of the five-bear family in Alaska.

LaMotte was the only school I heard from after my gruesome mauling in Yellowstone. And hear from them I did. I received three care packages full of original creations by the kids. The notes I received while still in the Intensive Care Unit in Idaho Falls were particularly heartening. Richard and Ron read some to me:

Please recover quick so you can come back to our school again.

Forgive the grizzly.

Don't give up your dream.

One of the teachers made my day by sending this note:

My name is Jerry Brunt and I'm the 3rd/4th grade teacher at LaMotte School. Our students were very impressed by your presentation earlier in the year and we were all saddened to read about your recent injury. When the kids were told that you were hurt, a few were a bit frightened until someone mentioned that you wouldn't blame the bear. The conversation then turned more toward understanding that the bear was probably startled and that no one was to blame. It seems that your teaching is taking hold. Thank you.

The kids wanted to send you these letters, cards, and pictures and we hope they find your body healing and your spirits high. Our thoughts and prayers go out to you and your family.

Thank you, again, for all you do to help us become more thoughtful human beings. We look forward to seeing you in the future.

Five months after my mauling, when I was ready, there was no question about which school I would be returning to first. The trees were leafless and a winter chill wafted through the air as I pulled into the parking lot and unloaded my guitar. The entire school, teachers included, was waiting for me.

I opened with my song, "Wonderful World of Grizzly Bears," then proclaimed that it was no less of a wonderful world to me because of my accident. After an abbreviated version of my story, questions flowed for over an hour. The faces of the children showed intense interest and concern. Instead of asking for gory details, they asked things like, "Will you go back out there again?" "Do you still feel the same about grizzlies?" "Where do you like photographing better, Yellowstone or Alaska?" and "What will you do differently in the future?" A teacher asked what I would do if I could no longer take photographs, which at the time was unclear in her mind. I told the gathering that what I was doing right then—educating and answering questions—had been and always would be the most important work I could ever do, especially from that day forward.

At the conclusion of this special gathering, I shared handshakes and hugs with every child on the way out. Some spoke with me briefly. I was not in a hurry to leave. One of the children told a teacher, "He doesn't look much different except for his eye patch." Many of the kids said, "You must come back!" I felt like one more piece of my life had slipped back into place.

Afterword

So the silver-tipped monarch retreats to the mountains
With hard-earned wisdom, his memory long
As the wilderness goes, so goes the grizzly
Swept away, forever gone
Forever gone

—"Forever Gone," music and lyrics by James R. Cole

I WAS JUST STEPPING out of my van in the parking lot of
the Gold Strike Gift Shop in Gardiner, Montana, the active
border town at the north entrance to Yellowstone Park, sporting clean clothes after my first shower in six days. Then someone yelled "Jim!" As I looked to the left, Mark Miller—a friend,
Gardiner resident, and fellow wildlife photographer—stopped
and asked, "Did you know there is a grizzly in Gardiner?" I
said "No," but my gears abruptly shifted as I jumped back into
the van and followed him across town.

We couldn't spot the bear at first but he finally came into

view, moving steadily to the east above us through the open rocky sagebrush northeast of town. The bear traveled below and around two big homes high on a hillside north of Gardiner then down into a draw (a dry streambed) where he located an old deer carcass.

Jim Miller (no relation to Mark) from Montana Fish, Wildlife and Parks was on the scene to make sure the bruin was heading out of town. The bear soon left the emaciated carcass then headed up toward the Tavertine Road where Jim, myself, and a couple of others had parked our cars. Jim asked that we all stay back to let the young bruin cross the road in front of the vehicles so that he could fire a cracker shell behind its path to startle the bear and compel it to proceed further into the backcountry and further from potential trouble.

It wasn't long before the grizzly climbed up to the road and warily crossed in front of us. As he began his ascent up the steep hillside, Jim fired one cracker shell. The bear immediately reacted by running up and over the hill, frequently looking back but quickly putting more and more distance between himself and us humans and our noisy machines far below. With Yellowstone's Electric Peak as a backdrop, we saw the young bear's pace slow as he continued eastward toward Eagle Creek Campground. An older couple exited a campsite as the bear approached their fire grate, picnic table, and white van. The couple stood and watched with Jim and a small gathering crowd as the bruin walked and sniffed his way through the occupied campsite. These campers had done a good job, leaving no food scraps or intriguing smells for this bear to find. Responsible camping goes a long way toward avoiding human/bear problems.

The bear soon disappeared into dense underbrush nearby, took a brief soak in Eagle Creek (it was a hot spring afternoon) and emerged shaking off the water like a wet dog. Jim watched carefully as the grizzly began foraging through green spots on the other side of the creek; he wanted to make sure that this animal was moving away from the campground and thus from human-occupied areas. Showing the insight and understanding that makes him an excellent wildlife official, Jim later confided to me that from a standpoint of human safety, he was far more concerned about a well-known and particularly belligerent bison bull who was napping nearby than this passive young grizzly.

Jim fired another cracker into the area near the bear. The noisy rifle shell seemed to have little effect; the bruin fled just a short distance. The animal slowly continued his trek north along Eagle Creek and away from the campground as Jim and the other onlookers headed back toward town. I thanked Jim for handling the situation so well, understanding that this mellow bear did not pose a threat but just needed to learn to steer clear of developed areas. He had gotten his lesson and hopefully would not return.

After all the human commotion had died down, I further observed this bear with binoculars on his journey north along the creek. He munched on lush green grasses while slowly moving uphill through dense cover toward a switchback along a winding gravel road. What a sight as he stood to watch a slow-moving vehicle pass by, then stopped to dig up a nest of scurrying pocket gophers. Mighty shoulder muscles allow grizzlies to dig relentlessly when the opportunity for a subterranean feast presents itself.

The bear kept moving and munching through these wide-open sagebrush hills, stopping once on a big boulder to look back like a king surveying his domain. Later, the bear switched gears and headed purposefully downhill back toward the Jardine Road. He interrupted his route twice to nibble on the dry tops of sagebrush bushes. As far as I know, these sagebrush bushes are not bear food and do not provide any significant nutrition. However, grizzlies commonly dig around them for pocket gophers and their caches and feed on seasonal vegetation in their midst. I have observed grizzlies biting the tops of this abundant and fragrant shrubbery on three occasions; all three times the sessions were brief, humans were nearby, and the bears appeared to be mildly stressed. My theory is that sagebrush munching is a sign of low-level stress and agitation, though it remains just a theory.

As he reached the dirt road, the grizzly stopped to wait for a car to pass, like a wary human pedestrian waiting at a crosswalk. He looked around while crossing, then disappeared into the evening shadows on the other side.

In places like Gardiner, humans and bears have learned to co-exist with reasonable success out of necessity; each depends on the other. But in most other parts of this country, the drive to develop and the irrational fear of the bear tends to win out. My great fear, and the fear of many naturalists and environmentalists, is that the story of the California grizzly may be playing out again in the West of modern times.

California was probably the most bountiful grizzly bear habitat of all time. In the temperate climate, many bears had no need to hibernate thanks to the plentiful food available year-round. Although very little recorded data exists, before white men migrated to the region in significant numbers beginning in the mid-1800s, the territory boasted an enormously healthy population of huge, fat bruins, estimated to be about 10,000. But the combination of gold, luxurious weather, and fertile soil also represented a prime target for relentless westward migration. Unlike the native peoples, white men chose to exterminate rather than live with the great bear, a job made easier with the advent of the repeating rifle. The California grizzly was rendered extinct in a mere sixty years and has been gone now for almost a century. Its likeness continues to decorate the state flag, a reminder of what could have been.

The changes occurring today in grizzly country remind us that if the plentiful California grizzly could be wiped out, no bear is safe. When I moved to Bozeman, Montana, back in 1998, I could see a lot of wild country from my windows. I live a simple life; if someone were to break into my house and rob me blind, all he'd get would be my guitar, my camera, and my computer. That would be painful for me, and I would feel violated, but it wouldn't be much of a haul compared to what a thief might find in most of the new homes popping up like weeds here in western Montana. I prefer to live lightly on the land and although I am a consumer and admittedly part of the problem, I leave a relatively a small footprint on Mother Earth. I would rather spend my time watching the wild panorama out my windows or walking in it with my own feet than spending considerable time vegging out in front of the tube.

The trouble is, there's a lot less wild country here these days. According to the U.S. Census Bureau, four of the fastest growing metro areas in the country are in what they call the "Intermountain West." My county, Gallatin County, is one of the fastest growing in the state and the nation. For some places—such as Boulder, Colorado, my home for many years—it's too late for wilderness and grizzlies. To control relentless growth, many years ago Boulder came up with a master plan to protect its remaining open space. The city drew a line at the edge of the foothills that essentially said, *"No mas."* All land west of that line was designated as greenbelt with no further development allowed. The area now supports a wide variety of wildlife, including mountain lions and an increased population of black bears.

The city did the best it could—after the fact. Now the sprawl is forced to spread east. For all its dramatic mountain scenery and superb grizzly bear habitat, the last known silvertip in Colorado was killed in 1979.

Bozeman has no master plan at this time. They are talking about subdivisions in the mountains, around the city, and they are already changing the land forever. I am seeing the same symptoms I lived through in Boulder. People are buying land in the middle of prime wildlife habitat, building a house, then watching another house go up next to them, then another, and before you realize it, the land is scarred and the habitat has been permanently compromised.

Time was, not too many years ago, that I could go for my morning walks south of town and look forward to the same glorious vistas; after years, they became like old friends I would get excited about seeing as I rounded a bend in the trail. Now my attitude is different because in walking some of my old, best-worn trails I'm afraid of what I'm going to find. I'm not exaggerating when I tell you that I can walk a trail, go back out on the same trail two weeks later and find new roads, fire hydrants, and huge homes sprouting like wild mushrooms from the pristine landscape.

Another disturbing change: once upon a time, you would see very little construction in winter in this part of the country. It was just too darned snowy and cold. Outdoor work would shut down until at least spring, and sometimes spring took its time in coming. Now, as a result of climate change, I see construction activity year-round, even in winter. That was unheard of until not too long ago. The same change is bringing more and more people to this area to live. For many years, all but the hardiest were kept away by the long, hard winters that we used to get in these parts. Not anymore. Now the winters aren't quite as harsh, and that is increasing the pressure to populate and develop in western Montana—one of the last places in the Lower 48 where people can find space and wild country and the way of life they dream about.

That sounds nice and libertarian and all, except for the fact that what started out as a Manifest Destiny dream is becoming a nightmare for the grizzly bear, the wilderness as a whole, and ultimately for us. When does it stop? At what point do we allow the population in the Lower 48 to grow so much and spread so widely that there are no more grizzly bears and no more wilderness? Wilderness is defined as country where the hand of man cannot be easily perceived. Other than road and trail systems and minimally developed areas, that description works for much of the land in Glacier and Yellowstone National Parks. But as we expand relentlessly into the so-called "last wild places" on the periphery of these two great national parks, wilderness is in danger of becoming something that's confined to the history books. As someone who cherishes not only the great grizzly bear but the untrammeled country that it calls its home, I think it's important to close this book with a discussion of what's at stake and how we might still throw a "Hail Mary" pass to the grizzly before it's too late.

To begin, why is the grizzly so important in the first place? I would love to argue the point from my perspective: that grizzly bears and the wild lands that are their kingdom are worth preserving forever for their own sakes, that we shouldn't need any justification for making lands off limits to any development (including roads) beyond the fact that the bears are magnificent, unique creatures and incredible examples of what nature can do when she's inspired. That is how I feel, but

I know that's not a realistic justification. Many Americans hate and fear grizzlies and see the wilderness as something to exploit, subdivide, and tame. If they experience wild country at all, they'd rather do it from the back seat of a car or in a wild animal park. Millions of others genuinely care about bears and conservation, but when it comes to choosing between their property rights and grizzlies, property is usually the winner.

To make the case for preservation in a way that acknowledges these facts, we have to start by looking at the value of the grizzly in the terms by which most people measure value: economic. Around the world, ecotourism is becoming a multibillion dollar industry, and the big, charismatic predators—lions, tigers, and bears, to borrow a line from a film—are some of the most popular attractions. One of the benefits of the grizzly bear is that it can spark sustainable economic growth in communities that surround prime habitat. Exploiting natural resources is incredibly expensive. Energy companies, loggers, and builders not only have to navigate years-long approval processes, but they inevitably have to deal with lawsuits as well. Properly promoted and experienced in a low-impact way, a thriving grizzly population in an unbelievably beautiful natural setting currently helps to bring a steady infusion of tourist dollars to bear-rich ecosystems while costing relatively little to develop. Plus, there's the advantage that unlike trees or coal, if protected and respected, the bears will not run out.

In Alaska, residents are beginning to see the economic value of bears. For state natives, bears can be hunted inside and outside of the national parks and preserves. But if you come from outside the state and you want to hunt bears, you are required to hire a resident guide, which costs an arm and a leg. This is especially true on Kodiak Island, where the biggest and most desirable trophy bears are to be found and where a hunt can cost up to $20,000.

Now, I don't jump for joy at the idea of any bear hunting. But even without pressure from environmentalists, the economic benefits are beginning to open eyes that grizzlies may be worth more alive than dead. I see people voting for "bear tourism" with their pocketbooks. Bear viewers are coming up to Alaska, renting hotels, planes, guides, and cars, spending small fortunes being flown into grizzly-dense areas just for a day so they can get pictures and have the experience of a lifetime. The idea isn't quite as applicable to the Lower 48, because we don't have the dense salmon areas where lots of bears congregate. But slowly, communities in bear ecosystems are starting to realize that these gorgeous, charismatic creatures are a magnet for city dwellers who are hungry for an experience that appeals to something primal in all of us.

However, the most persuasive reason in my mind for changing our attitudes toward the grizzly is that it is in our own survival interest. Grizzlies are the harbingers of wild country, and their health reflects the health of the entire ecosystem. They are the monarchs of the American West. We have much in common with the bears, as it turns out. We are both at the top of our respective food chains, and we both depend on the health of the earth to sustain us. As our population grows and our climate changes, we depend on the great untouched wild lands of the West to help moderate the swings in our weather. More to the point, if we open these lands to development and pave over much of what was once forest, meadow, and river bottom, we could accelerate a potential climate catastrophe. The survival of the wild is our survival as well.

But let's say that it's not that dire, that climate change won't be that dramatic. We still need wilderness for our mental health. Henry David Thoreau wrote in *Walden:* "I went to the woods because I wished to live deliberately, to front only the essential facts of life, and see if I could not learn what it had to teach, and not, when I came to die, discover that I had not lived." Edward Abbey wrote: "Wilderness is not a luxury but a necessity of the human spirit." There is something in us that needs green space, untamed country, and the mystery of deep forests far from the noises made by humans.

If you breathe easier when you take even a short walk in the woods by your home, you know what I mean. Most of us lead lives defined by busy schedules and being "on call"; I know because I was once in that same boat. Because of this, even people who live in huge cities and see the wilderness only through photos in *National Geographic* take solace in knowing the wild country is there—that grizzlies and wolves and mountain lions roam free. That knowledge is like a safety valve; it makes the stresses in our lives more tolerable.

Thanks to the environmental movement that has surfaced in recent decades, our species has shown the wisdom and restraint to protect magnificent creatures and their equally magnificent homes. We need wilderness to keep us sane. Protecting grizzlies is protecting ourselves. The wild lands define who we are as a people. They are essential for our spirit, our soul. I don't have kids, but I want your kids and grandkids to come to Yellowstone and Glacier and see the great bears in the grandeur of their natural habitat, not just read about how they used to roam the parks and see bears in zoos.

The defining question of our time is whether we will keep acting with wisdom and restraint. I think it is clear that humans need grizzly bears and the ecosystems they represent, but the question is, will we have the foresight and political will to act on that fact? Will we stop squeezing the edges of grizzly country and shrinking their habitat? Are we going to allow wild country to continue to exist? We have that power. The fate of the grizzly is in our hands.

I see this as a question of freedom versus values. We value personal freedom above everything else in this country. But we have to ask ourselves at this point in history, does that include the freedom to thoughtlessly destroy our environment and possibly imperil ourselves? The other freedom that is dangerous to our environment is our feeling that we own and control the land and can do with it as we please. We crave land, especially land that we feel we have dominion over. What do you tell the guy from New Jersey who wants to buy fifty acres of land in Montana so he can escape the city and live according to his own "live free or die" ethic? You certainly can't tell him that he cannot buy the land because it is in critical wildlife habitat. Do you tell him that he's buying in prime grizzly territory? If he already knows that, how do we know his intentions? People want land, and there isn't much that can stop them from claiming that land—and potentially wiping out everything else that's not of their design—when they get it.

Political forces at work in Alaska represent the best and worst of this movement. Even with the vast wilderness that some see as "unlimited," and the rise of eco-tourism, most conservationists see the trend of development going in the same direction as elsewhere. In Alaska and other resource-rich areas, we have the freedom to live where we want, but how do we live responsibly? We are the stewards, and we need to show some responsibility. All too often, our approach is that the resource is there for us to use and that's all that matters. That's why I think the answer doesn't lie just in changing laws but in changing *attitudes* and *values*.

The freedoms we have must come with responsibility. As part of the national movement for wilderness preservation, we need to stop making wilderness a political issue and make it a human issue. We need to develop more humility. We seem to feel entitled to step on the throat of the natural world—to live where we want and how we want—when we should feel grateful to have this country with all its resources and to live on this land that feeds and clothes us. We need to learn from the natural world rather than thoughtlessly extract from it and permanently scar it. It is time for a change in our personal values. Our values need to become about *stewardship* of the land, not private ownership. We can work with people who love the land—from biologists and naturalists to ranchers and hunters—as long as they want to respect and preserve it, not exploit it.

A great example was the delisting of the grizzly in the Greater Yellowstone Ecosystem. In this area, hunting organizations were salivating to get guns in their hands and kill grizzly bears. This is a bizarre and savage reaction of people who want to exercise power over nature. We're not talking about subsistence hunting; this is murdering for a trophy and a macho feather in one's cap. That is their value system: crush what they don't control for self-interest. Bears are beautiful and peace-loving, and I can say that as someone who potentially has more reason than anyone to fear and hate them. Based on the mistakes of the past, wouldn't it make more sense to maintain the legal protection for grizzlies until we are positive that the population is healthy and stable, rather than bowing to political pressure?

There certainly are some signs that awareness is growing. At a public meeting about delisting, I got up and spoke from written notes for my three-minute allotment. Prepared text isn't my style, but I had much to cover and I made my points. A biologist came all the way from British Columbia to Bozeman for his three minutes, to say that he was strongly against delisting. He said, "I'm seeing the progression here, the migration west from the east coast and Midwest. Now Montana is getting too developed. I see British Columbia being a generation or two behind you, but I see all the same patterns—all the mistakes being made. I see the same thing coming a generation or so later to southern British Columbia." He was seeing the inevitable progression of population North and West, with the same earmarks: habitat destruction and development. We need more people speaking out about the fact that we cannot continue to expand and expand like we have.

On September 21, 2009, a federal judge restored the threatened status of the grizzly under the Endangered Species Act, stating that the bears remain at risk. This is good news, but it will remain a hot-button political issue for a long time to come.

We see land and ownership of land as signs of wealth as well as a legacy to pass on. But if we're going to arrest the progress of this disease, our values need to change to where our idea of wealth includes balance, harmony, beauty, health, and respect for all living things. We need to get away from being obsessed with our individual possessions and take pride in our collective possession: the beautiful natural world and the creatures than inhabit it. As long as money and land are more important to us than beauty, health, and preservation, we will be about consumption and destruction, not healing.

During the time this book was being written, this nation was undergoing the harshest economic collapse since the Great Depression. But surely you know the saying, "It's an ill wind that blows no one any good." Even in a terrible recession, some good can be found. One blessing is this: development has come to a temporary standstill. We are being given a brief window of time to question the values that got us here. But we only have a short time. As we try to restart the stalled economy, rampant development may start up again. It's during this time that we have an opportunity to take a step back and consider transforming our values.

One way to begin is to change the way that the media and the Park Service treat the subject of bears and bear attacks. The media treats every bear attack with sensationalism, because the media thrives on bad news. If a local TV station can shout, "Grizzly mauls hiker!" it's going to get better ratings. If someone receives minor injuries, it usually grabs headlines ahead of a fatality caused by something less exotic. But with the Park Service, the misinformation is really inexcusable. Their efforts to keep bears and people apart are certainly well-intentioned. But the way they lecture about bear dangers and post massive amounts of fearful and cautionary information about bear attacks in Yellowstone, you would think infants were being pulled screaming from their cars by raging grizzlies. As I pointed out earlier, many more people have died from falls and drowning in Yellowstone than bear attacks. But again, not much is said about the less sensational dangers of Yellowstone.

The Park Service has people who come in for a few seasons, get a few weeks of training, and then are asked every question in the book about grizzlies, bison, local biology, thermal features, and so on, and they don't always have the right answers. I'm appalled at the amount of misinformation that's given out about grizzlies in our national parks. I have personally seen naturalists in Glacier and Yellowstone not be able to distinguish between a grizzly bear and a black bear and mis-identify the bears to tourists.

The Native Americans proved that we can live with the grizzly. Some hunted them; most did not. The bear was their brother. The grizzly bear shaman was the most respected and powerful shaman in native culture. Their disciples realized that the grizzly is a peace-loving animal and they found ways to coexist. We can do this if we so choose. It will take a lot of effort, but it can be done.

Now we have a mix of people on the land. Some will live with bears, properly handle attractants, and put up electric fencing to keep them out, although this is not possible with huge ranches. Then you have people who cannot be convinced that the bear is anything more than a varmint. They fear the bear and hate what they fear. Theirs is the stubborn, set-in-stone attitude: "My grandfather and great grandfather did this, I won't change." Some ranchers say, "If we lose a few cattle to predators, we can accept it because that's the price of living in harmony in this incredible country." Others scream that bears and wolves are vermin and they resent the government pro-tecting and reintroducing them. The second group can't be convinced. But there are a lot of people who I believe have open minds and can be convinced with simple common sense education.

You deal with the vermin group by creating strict rules about what can and can't be done in bear country. If they can't abide by the rules, it will become very expensive to run their ranches. Rules should be strict and strictly enforced, because most problems are the humans' fault. The people I know who live successfully in grizzly country have applied very strict rules they follow, and they have relatively few problems.

Things are starting to change, slowly. Now you have wildlife managers and ranchers who isolate cattle carcasses in specific areas away from the public so the grizzlies can feed off them and stay away from the healthy cattle. There are some bear specialists who work with local communities and ranchers when they have problems with grizzlies, even helping ranchers set up electric fences, which don't eliminate all problems but do reduce them. There are ranchers doing great preventive work in bear territory. Ted Turner owns a massive ranch near Bozeman. His ranch protects everything, including wolves and bears. In fact, people have come to his property to study wolves. That's what we need more of. The more people who own property in wild country, love living among grizzly bears, and take steps to protect both their own property and the welfare of the bears, the better.

The question is, in this brief window that we've been granted by the economic downturn, can we speed up the change of values?

I believe that we should aggressively protect more land, and do it in a way that doesn't seesaw back and forth with each new presidential administration. We should make protection permanent. The simple fact is that with all the generous ranchers and good intentions, if we did not have the national parks and their supporting boundary areas like national forests and private lands, there would be no grizzly bears or wild country—and the same is true for wolves, wolverines, and lynx. We want to protect the land, but there's a balance between that and using the land. It's the mission of the Park Service: to preserve the resource for its own sake but also for the enjoyment of the people. Which comes first, the chicken or the egg? It's a tough balancing act.

We need to protect more land and we need to know which is most vital to protect. Glacier National Park and Yellowstone National Park are already protected, and they are the centerpieces for the Northern Continental Divide Ecosystem and the Greater Yellowstone Ecosystem, respectively. Those ecosystems spread out to many national forests, wilderness areas, and thousands of acres of private land. These are the primary remaining grizzly bear habitats south of the Canadian border. Other fragmented habitat remains in far northwest Montana, Idaho, and northern Washington. But the heart of what's left is in these two regions.

The Nature Conservancy is doing great work, especially on the Rocky Mountain Front, which is part of the Northern Continental Divide Ecosystem (NCDE). The Front runs about 300 miles along the eastern edge of the NCDE and up into Canada. It harbors the last remaining "plains" grizzlies. Long ago, grizzlies were plains animals, walking in the open spaces, and this is one of the reasons they developed the protective instincts they did, because they were out in the open so much. On the Front, we still have some plains grizzlies. Though they don't spend all their lives on the plains, they are going back to old habits: traveling east to find chokecherries and other berries and sniffing out livestock carcasses like they did naturally with bison carcasses in these very same areas in the distant past.

Two decades ago, the Nature Conservancy purchased 15,000 acres northwest of Great Falls, Montana, which has become the Pine Butte Swamp Preserve. Since then, it has acquired additional land and conservation easements from adjacent landowners, adding another 3,000 acres and protecting this vitally important area for all time.

Pine Butte Swamp Preserve is a lush lowland extension of the Bob Marshal Wilderness, the convergence of the mountains and plains, and the largest wetland complex along the Front. The threat of oil and gas development looms, so the master plan is to secure substantially more habitat used most heavily by grizzlies. This is a superb but restricted hiking area; I once got permission to walk this land and to study the bear ecology. This critical grizzly bear habitat is unique, important, and must be protected.

What would I do if I had my way? I would expand Yellowstone and Glacier, expand wilderness areas, and create iron-clad buffer zones to protect wilderness and wild ecosystems from any kind of development in perpetuity. I would also encourage the hiring of more trained local personnel to work as conservationists among landowners and ranchers. There's a guy who lives and works with the ranchers on the Rocky Mountain Front who's terrific, because even though he may have philosophical differences with some landowners, he's

one of them. He knows them and understands their challenges. He's able to respect their points of view and works
with them very well. He knows when to push and when to
pull. That's the kind of relationship we've got to have between
landowners and regulators: partnership, not confrontation.
People want to feel part of a solution, not over-regulated by
the government. Local people working one-on-one with local
people is one way to accomplish this.

But for me, everything begins with education. We need
much more compelling public education to help adults and especially kids understand the truth about grizzly bears and
their habitat. Kids can see the wonder of these animals much
more than adults because they haven't learned yet to fear them
or to lust for their land. This has always been the heart and
soul of my work: to teach young people the truth about bears
and that we can live with them, so when they grow up they
will support more ecosystem conservation.

Education is the key to defusing the fear, because our fear
of grizzlies is irrational. For example, there were ninety-eight
deaths due to motorcycle accidents in Colorado in 2008; there
were three deaths due to bear attacks in the entire country in
2008, and one of those was a trained movie bear that killed his
handler. Did people stop riding motorcycles? Of course they
didn't. But with bears, you are in the wilderness, out of your
comfort zone, and somewhere out there lurks a creature that
is far bigger and more powerful than you are, that has huge
canine teeth and can run as fast as a racehorse, and you don't
understand it, so you fear it. As of this writing, there have

been no bear-related human fatalities in Yellowstone since 1986. You're in more danger walking the streets of Manhattan any night of the week than you are in Yellowstone. But too many people don't see it that way.

How do we change values? We get people reading books like this. I speak to schools and try to answer every last question from kids as well as teachers. If we get to children early, we can change how they think about bears in the future. But you're dealing with some kids whose parents are telling them other things, and this is where my music is important. Songs really drive home the message. But it's important to get to the parents, because they are the biggest influences on their kids, so I do adult and family educational programs as well. If I can convince some parents and a lot of kids, I'm making a difference.

Just over a year after the attack, I was sitting on a high ridge in Hayden Valley watching a grizzly eating grasses down below near a thermal area. The young bruin was flanked by two bison and looked very small by comparison. I was eating an energy bar and watching the bear when my eye caught movement in the sagebrush about halfway down the ridge. I picked up my binoculars and saw the beautiful faces of a mother grizzly and one yearling cub. Based on my knowledge of the bears that I have seen in the valley over the past two years, I was sure that she was the one that had mauled me. We were only a little over a mile from the attack site, and I was genuinely happy to see her again.

As I reached for my camera, both mother and cub caught my scent and majestically stood, looking right into my eyes.

I was shaking with excitement, but I didn't feel a sliver of fear. This was not a surprise point blank encounter, so I was completely at ease. I never stood up or reached for my bear spray. I wanted to watch these beautiful animals and not spook them if I could help it.

I'm not sure if she actually saw me, but it didn't take the mother bear long to determine the direction of the intrusive scent. Both bears dropped back down on all fours, turned around, and galloped away. Other than stopping twice to look back, they barely broke stride before disappearing into the thermal forest. It was a truly exhilarating moment for me and gave me a sense of closure I hadn't known I needed.

I have spent over thirty years in the field, but field time and photography are not nearly as important now as my mission to help save the grizzly bears and the environment and give people the right perspective on nature and ourselves. I want to do everything I can with all the tools I have. The more we understand, the more we will be humble. The humbler we are, the more receptive the general public will be to laws and regulations and a new set of values. But there are few people who can share this understanding—not from having taken a class given by a government agency, but by actually being out there and having lived it and seen it firsthand. That's what I've done. I feel very fortunate. I owe a huge debt for my great life experience with the grizzly in his spectacular wilderness home. I could never fully repay this debt, but I take the responsibility seriously. And let me tell you, if I wasn't humbled by all that I have seen, I would truly be blind.